Entrepreneur MAGAZINE'S **Expert**_Advice_

Franchises
& Business
Opportunities

ANDREW A. CAFFEY

EP
Entrepreneur. Press

D0907368

Managing Editor: Jere Calmes
Cover Design: Dunn and Associates
Composition and Production: Eliot House Productions

Library of Congress Cataloging-in-Publication Data
Caffey, Andrew A.
    Franchises & business opportunities: how to find, buy, and operate a
    successful business/by Andrew A. Caffey.
        p. cm.
    Includes index.
    ISBN 1-891984-41-1
        1. Franchises (Retail trade)—United States. I. Title: Franchises and
    business opportunities. II. Title.
    HF5429.235.U5 C34 2002
    658.8'708—dc21   2001040643

Printed in Canada

09 08 07 06 05 04 03 02 01 10 9 8 7 6 5 4 3 2 1

Franchises
& Business
Opportunities

CONTENTS

DEDICATION

This book is dedicated to Nancy, Alex, Brian,
and, of course, Katie—lights of my life.

INTRODUCTION

If you have picked up this book with a thought of getting into business for yourself, *congratulations*! Business ownership has rewards that those in more traditional walks of employee life will never experience. Through business ownership lifelong dreams are realized. This is especially true in times of uncertainty and national struggle. The events of September 11 and their aftermath have led many Americans to reassess their lives and their dreams. Punching a time clock will *never* compare to the thrill of receiving your first client payment or of watching your business' sales numbers climb higher and higher from one month to the next.

Besides the incentive of fortunes waiting to be made, there are also distinct side benefits of owning your own business. Your time becomes your own, you might be able to work out of your house, leave behind that hideous commute, and maybe you'll see more of your family. The side benefits become all the more attractive in difficult times.

Franchise and business opportunity investments are the first rungs of the business ownership ladder. They offer to the business novice the prospect of a comfortable entry into business ownership, where experienced help and advice are available, and where someone has already worked out the bugs. If that notion is appealing to you, read on. You have your nose in the right book.

Franchise and business opportunities are business packages that allow you to own your own business and be in business for yourself (not "by yourself," as the franchisors say). They are both offered by sellers on this same basic premise: "We have already devised a successful business program for you, and for your investment we will provide you all the tools you need to own and operate your own successful business."

Of course, these packages may also pose a threat to the novice who does not have the experience to see around the next business corner. Don't kid yourself: there are huge risks in buying business packages. This is particularly true of business opportunities because they are not regulated under state and federal law to the same degree as franchising is. But high risk is also a part of starting a business concept completely on your own. After all, *financial risk* defines the lives of entrepreneurs; it invigorates them and drives them to achieve and succeed. Business owners live with financial risk in their lives every day, and this is also increasingly true for employees. "Job security" for employees is fast becoming an oxymoron. Your task in investing in a franchise or business opportunity is to manage and minimize the risk as much as possible.

That is where this book comes in. You need to protect yourself, spend your money wisely, find the right fit for your particular needs and desires, and know how to evaluate the hundreds of investment opportunities available in the marketplace. You have in your hands the information you need to understand the process, spot a phony offering, ask the right questions, and avoid many of the traps that catch novice investors. All this will help you find that great business franchise package or business opportunity to launch your career as an independent business owner.

This exploration of the world of franchise and business opportunities is organized around my fundamental approach to investing in business packages: self-evaluation, a disciplined approach to the hunt, a vigorous gathering and assessment of available information, detailed discussions with existing owners, and careful use of professional assistance when appropriate. Take a careful approach to your investment with this guidance, and I hope you will be well on your way to a great business experience.

Enjoy the journey!

—A.A. Caffey

PART I

SETTING UP
FOR
YOUR BUSINESS

SO YOU WANT TO OWN YOUR OWN BUSINESS?

*A*T THE AGE OF *30,* SUCCESS WAS ELUDING JON, AND HE KNEW *something was wrong. After a promising high school athletic career and a fair academic showing at his state's university, he bounced from one job to the next with no sense of purpose and without achieving the success he knew was in him. People liked him, and he was presentable, but his 30th birthday stopped him in his tracks. How and when was he going to realize his potential? He hungered for success but didn't quite know how to go about it. Somehow that part was not taught in school.*

BUSINESS OWNERSHIP

The Advantages

Owning your own business—a sparkling, elusive goal of the American dream. It wasn't until Jon began considering starting his own business that he felt some optimism about his life's goals.

Business ownership seems out of reach to many would-be entrepreneurs because it appears expensive, complicated, and intimidating. Yet, business ownership is the most common route taken by Americans to substantial wealth.

There are a number of advantages to owning a business:

- Small business ownership can bring *independence*; no more punching a time clock and worrying whether your job will be there tomorrow.
- It can mean *flexibility* so that you are free to take time off and spend time with the ones you love.
- It can bring a *healthy variety* of daily tasks instead of the repetitive routines of so many workplace specialties.
- Business ownership can bring immense *pride in accomplishment*.
- Business owners make a *difference* in the lives of everyone involved, especially employees who depend on the owner's business savvy to keep their jobs.
- Owning your own business gives you the chance to do it *your way*. It gives you the chance to bring your pride, your style, your gifts to a business operation.
- Business ownership can bring *wealth*. You don't need to be Bill Gates to realize the rewards of starting your own business. Ownership gives you the opportunity to build equity value over time, so that once your business is up and running, it will have acquired a substantial value. It puts to shame the apparent value of a week-to-week paycheck after those taxes are taken out.

The Challenges

Given these benefits, why don't even more people own their own businesses? It takes an enormous amount of work, perseverance, and drive to overcome the challenges of getting started. To many people, those challenges can seem insurmountable. Just take a look at what it was like for Jon:

Jon had a fevered panic dream: Look at this checklist of things I have to do! I can't do this! It's a mess. Borrow a quarter million dollars? Who is going to lend me that kind of dough? Quit my job and launch out on my own? What if I fail? The national failure rates for small businesses are staggering. Am I nuts?! Even if I find the money I will have to learn the traps of the business. Sure, there are lots of other businesses in my line I could talk to, but they are all competitors! No way are they going to tell me how to run one of these operations. I have to hire people, buy advertising, buy inventory… I don't know how to do that. I'll probably get ripped off at every turn and lose my shirt.

In some ways, Jon is right. It is difficult to find the information you need to set up and operate a business, create the trademark and graphics, and amass the cash and borrowed funds necessary to get going. As they say, if it were easy, everyone would do it.

But owning a successful business is possible and there are many ways to go about doing it. One way is to buy a franchise. The franchise concept is designed to help the average person overcome the challenges of small business ownership and get into a proven business, while providing the type of training and continued coaching that is not available anywhere else.

Another route is to buy a business opportunity venture. This is similar to a franchise in that it is a packaged business kit, usually for a purchase price that will fit on a credit card. The right business opportunity is a type of investment that has many pluses and minuses.

There are lots of ways to skin the business cat, of course. Whether you choose a franchise, a business opportunity, or something else entirely, it must be a program that fits your needs and gets you on the road to building wealth through small business ownership.

The meaning of "franchise" and a "business opportunity" will be discussed, so don't worry about it if they are unfamiliar terms. For many people the image of a McDonald's® restaurant comes to mind when someone says "franchise," because McDonald's is such a successful franchise concept. But there are lots of other franchise programs to look into, and a lot of them outside of the food business. This book will talk about business opportunity programs, too. Business opportunity programs are generally not associated with a well known trademark, so think small, work-at-home business package.

SUMMARY NOTES

- Avenues to success are often not taught in our schools.
- Business ownership is a proven pathway to success and wealth.
- You can overcome the intimidating challenges of business ownership.
- Two popular ways to get into business are owning a franchise or a business opportunity package.

ACTION PLAN

Write down on a single sheet of paper three goals of a business you would start. How do you imagine it would change your life? Then write down three aspects of business that appeal to you. If you have any general ideas of the type of business that would appeal to you, note them on the same sheet. Keep this paper in a folder labeled "Business Planning;" you will want to refer to it again.

2

ORGANIZING FOR BUSINESS

*O*NCE *MERRY DECIDED TO GET INTO BUSINESS FOR HERSELF, SHE realized that she didn't know much about business organization. She had heard the scare stories: a friend's dad had lost everything in a stupid business concept, and because of the liabilities of the business failure, the friend and her family had to move out of their house and into an apartment when she was in high school. Merry was determined to be smart about her own business, protect herself as best she could, and build an organization that could stand on its own feet. However, despite her firm resolve, she didn't even know what questions to ask to get started.*

ADVANTAGES AND DISADVANTAGES OF DIFFERENT
BUSINESS ORGANIZATIONS

One of the early decisions all business people have to make is how best to organize legally to be in business. Do you form a corporation? Do you have to? Are there other choices? This can be confusing if you are new to business ownership. There are lots of choices and a number of concerns to consider as you sift through the options.

You can operate as a sole proprietor, a corporation, a partnership, or a limited liability company. Whether you select a franchise or a business opportunity, you need to select a form of business organization. Take a look at each one.

The Sole Proprietorship

A *sole proprietorship* is a business owned directly by one person. This is the simplest type of business organization, and some may even find it hard to think of it as an "organization." However, some sole proprietorships may be large and complex with many employees. For now think of a sole proprietorship as one person running the business as both owner and manager.

The greatest *advantage* to running the sole proprietorship is the ease with which it is formed. There are no papers to file or meetings to hold in order to keep it in existence. From an organizational point of view, you may simply start doing business as a sole proprietor with no further legal maintenance required. Of course there may be licenses or permits required for the type of business you are starting, but the "organization" of your business is done.

The greatest *disadvantage* of the sole proprietorship is personal liability. The owner is required to repay any amount borrowed personally no matter what happens to the business. This means they could lose more than their initial investment. There is no distinction between business and personal assets. A bank or other creditor may try to collect any money owed from the sole proprietor's personal assets if the business fails. You may obtain liability insurance, but it will not cover you if your business fails.

Another serious limitation for a sole proprietor is the inability to take on investors or partners. This may be unimportant for many businesses, but could make all the difference in financing others.

A lot of businesses start out as sole proprietorships and then morph into corporations or limited liability companies (LLCs). If you are buying a franchise, however, it may be important to consider forming a separate legal entity before you sign on to the franchised business because it can be difficult to transfer the franchise rights to your new entity after you sign the franchise agreement.

Partnership

A *partnership* exists when two or more people agree to run a business together and share control and profits. Creating a partnership does not require any formal steps. The agreement to form a partnership may be either expressed or implied, oral or written. However, it is highly recommended that a written partnership agreement be prepared and signed by the partners.

The partnership agreement should cover such issues as the amount of each partner's contribution, how profits will be shared, what authority each partner has, and how interests may be transferred. If a partnership is formed without a written agreement, the law will impose a series of standard terms that may not be intended by the partners. If you wish to have a partnership agreement, it is recommended that you consult with an attorney licensed in your state with some experience in the area.

Business partners should understand the significance the law places on sharing control. They may act on behalf of one another and the partnership in making agreements, incurring debt, and taking any other action in the course of running the business. The obligations of the business become personal to all. State law will impose equally shared liability on each general partner, unless the partnership agreement states otherwise. For example, if your partner takes out a loan on behalf of the business and the business fails, the bank will seek repayment from both your partner *and* you. If your partner or the partnership has no assets to satisfy the debt, the creditor may look to you personally.

So far we have been discussing a general partnership; however there is another form of partnership known as a *limited partnership*. A limited partnership has at least one general partner and one limited partner. The main difference between these two types of partners is that a limited partner has no liability for the debts of the partnership. Nor do they have rights to management or control of the business. The general partner controls the business and has unlimited liability. To form a limited partnership, you must carefully consult the laws of the state in which you do business and seek the assistance of a competent attorney. For accountability purposes, the partnership is required to report its income on IRS Form 1065.

Corporation

The *corporation* is radically different from the other forms of business organization. It is controlled by statute, and each state's laws vary to some extent. You should therefore contact the secretary of state's office in the state in which you incorporate for more information.

In the eyes of the law a corporation is a legal entity separate and apart from its shareholders. It may buy, sell, or inherit property, enter into contracts, and sue or be sued in court. It is also responsible for its own debts. If the corporation fails, creditors may not seek payment from investors in the company. The shareholder's liability is therefore limited to his or her initial investment.

Shareholders in a corporation are ultimately responsible for all corporate actions, somewhat like citizens in a democracy. Shareholders elect representatives to the board of directors and the board of directors appoints the officers of the corporation to handle its everyday affairs. This three-tier structure applies to nearly all corporations, from General Motors to the smallest one-owner, home-based corporation.

If you form a legal entity like a corporation or LLC, make sure that whenever you enter a business contract or other important obligation you bind the entity to the obligation and not yourself. To do this, make sure you sign in your official capacity showing your title, such as "President" or "Member." Make sure your title appears under your name and that you are committing the entity to the obligation.

Subchapter S Corporation

Most smaller businesses will benefit from selecting the tax treatment of an *subchapter S corporation*. A subchapter S corporation receives special tax treatment under the Internal Revenue Code and has some distinct advantages. These include:

- *No Double Taxation.* A subchapter S corporation sidesteps the principal disadvantage of the corporate form of doing business by receiving tax treatment that is similar to a partnership. It is not taxed at the corporate level, but the income of the entity is passed through to the shareholders and reported on each individual's personal tax return.
- *Ease of Election.* A new corporation or an existing corporation may elect subchapter S corporation treatment simply by filing IRS Form 2553.

In order to qualify for subchapter S corporation treatment, the corporation must be a domestic (U.S.) entity with one class of stock and no more than 35 shareholders. Its shareholders must be individuals, estates, or certain trusts and not other corporations. Finally, it may not have a nonresident alien among its shareholders. Most personally owned and family owned businesses qualify for subchapter S corporation treatment and should seriously consider electing it.

The drawback to a subchapter S corporation is that many of the corporate perks of a regular corporation may not be realized. For instance, a regular corporation can pay for the health plan of its shareholders, but a subchapter S corporation may not. There may be other drawbacks, as well, which you should review with your attorney.

Limited Liability Company

The limited liability company is a recently developed concept in business organization that has a number of advantages for small business owners. Like a subchapter S corporation, a limited liability company (LLC) offers the liability protection of a corporation and the tax benefits of a partnership, but does not require compliance with the legal formalities that characterize a corporation.

Wyoming first adopted an LLC statute in 1977, but the concept really caught on in the 1980s. In 1988, the IRS ruled that an LLC under Wyoming law would receive tax treatment like a partnership (on a pass-through basis to individual managers), and its popularity has since soared.

An LLC has an enormous advantage over the corporation: flexibility in its management. Depending on the particular requirements of your state's law, an LLC is operated by either members or by appointed or elected managers. It may be structured for governance and economics by agreement of its owner-members, and there are few limitations on the way it is organized and operated. Most new business owners are well advised to take a close look at the LLC concept.

For most small business owners, the answer will be to stay a sole proprietor (and run whatever liability risks there may be), create a corporation and elect subchapter S treatment under the Tax Code, or form a limited liability company. Buying a franchise will accelerate your decision making because the franchisor may demand you have your organization in place at the beginning of the franchise term.

CONCERNS UNDERLYING BUSINESS ORGANIZATIONS

In order to make the right choice of business organization, it is important to consider the following:

Personal Liability

If you do not form any legal entity to hold your business, you will be operating under your own name, as yourself, and putting your personal assets on the line. Your form of business ownership will be known as a "sole proprietor" and you will have no protection from claims anyone may have against your business.

Here's a quick example. You start a home business of buying and selling used video games. It takes off like a jack rabbit, and soon you are dealing in large wholesale lots of games. You enter into a contract with a new local games store to buy all of its used games for a year at a negotiated price, a contract that you estimate is worth $25,000. You do this because you have a buyer lined up who tells you he will buy as many games as you can produce for him.

One bleak day your buyer goes out of business, and disappears. The games store expects you to continue buying from them, but you don't have the cash or the buyers to move the merchandise. When you don't buy the used games as required in your contract, the seller files a lawsuit on the contract, seeking $25,000 in damages. Your lawyer tells you that because you operate as a sole proprietor, all of your personal assets are exposed to this claim, and you could lose your car and/or your house if you lose the case. If you operated as a corporation, he tells you, then it would be liable, and your personal assets would be out of your creditors' reach.

When someone talks about the disadvantages of operating under your own name, you need to weigh the potential liability that you could incur in the business. In large measure your decision depends on the type of business (will you be entering into contracts for substantial obligations?) and the state of your personal assets (can you absorb all potential losses of the business?).

Taxation

This is a biggie. There are dramatically different tax consequences depending on the form of business organization you use. Taxation concerns drive a lot of the business organization decisions, and some of the legal forms available strike a balance between liability and taxation.

If you operate as an individual sole proprietor, then your tax picture is straightforward. You simply add a Schedule C to your annual personal return.

Corporations have another story to tell. The law (and the IRS) recognize that a corporation is a separate entity and must pay *its own taxes* on its own net income. Then, when the corporation pays out a dividend to its owners, the owners must pay taxes on that income when they file their personal returns. In an important sense, a corporation is taxed twice: once on its own revenue, and again when the owners take money out of the corporation.

A traditional answer to this double whammy is an IRS tax treatment as a "subchapter S corporation." This is a corporation that has met a series of qualifications (mostly as to size and the number of shareholders) and has elected to receive special tax treatment. As a result, the subchapter S corporation has the liability protection of a standard corporation but is not taxed twice. The IRS allows the corporation to pass through its revenues to its owners and the taxation on that revenue at the owners' level. The subchapter S corporation does not pay taxes separately. The result: one time taxation. Problem solved.

A partnership has always been taxed directly to the individual partners; it is not considered a separate entity for liability or taxation purposes. Limited liability companies have also solved the taxation problem by receiving single tax treatment.

Flexibility

This concern becomes evident when you are told what directors and officers you must have and what annual meetings you must conduct in order to maintain a corporation. The law imposes rather extensive rules on the owners of a corporation, and if the rules are not followed, the liability shield effectiveness is lost. Partnerships are quite flexible. So are limited liability companies. Sole proprietorships are the most flexible of all, of course, because there is no organization to nurture along the way.

Flexibility has another dimension. Say you want to take in other owners and give them different shares of ownership. You cannot do that if you are a sole proprietor, but the other legal structures are designed for multiple owners.

SUMMARY NOTES

- Business organizations will change depending on the needs of the business itself and the organizers.
- Limiting personal liability, maximizing tax benefits, and flexibility are principal concerns.
- Understand the major forms of business organization before consulting with an attorney; it will save you time and money.
- One of the most attractive new forms of business organization is the limited liability company. It is fast becoming the leading choice of small business owners.

ACTION PLAN

Make a checklist of goals for your business as well as concerns you may have about things like ownership and liability. Take the list to a good attorney and ask what you need to do to form a solid business entity for your business plan.

PART II

THE GREAT
AMERICAN BUSINESS
OPPORTUNITY

THE BUSINESS OPPORTUNITY PACKAGE

IKE HAD A CAREER IN SOCIAL SERVICES THAT HE FOUND FUL-
filling, but it did not generate much of a paycheck.
He wanted to make additional money on his
weekends and evenings where he could work from his
house and have flexibility on the time commitment. A
friend told him that it sounded like he was looking for
a business opportunity program and encouraged Mike
to look into these programs. Mike thought it sounded
exactly like what he needed.

A business opportunity package does not lend itself to precise definition, unlike the more established business franchise. However, in general, *a business opportunity package is any set of goods or services offered by a seller that enables the purchaser to begin or maintain a business.* The concept covers franchises, multilevel marketing, and work-at-home piecework programs. Legal definitions are more precise, and we explore them in Chapter 4.

One classic business opportunity package is a string of vending machines, offered along with a promise that the seller will provide coaching on how to place the machines in profitable locations, maintain them, fill them with product, and collect the coins (the sexy part, right?). The seller may even offer to visit likely locations with the purchaser and provide direct, hands-on assistance.

> Location promises have been the source of a lot of problems in the business opportunity arena. Don't assume that the seller will be able to nail down good locations for vending devices.

A business opportunity may feature the offer and sale of any number of products and services, from women's hose to snack foods to trinkets to greeting cards. Recent technology developments have inspired numerous Internet and computer-based service concepts that fall under the business opportunity definition.

In contrast to a business franchise, no trademark is involved in a business opportunity transaction, nor is there a continuing commercial relationship between the purchaser and the seller. The purchaser is free to operate under any name, and the product or service sold is not usually identified by the seller's trademark. The seller exercises no "control" over the buyer's business operation. Where a franchisor makes sure you are operating exactly as prescribed, a business opportunity seller reserves no such right.

IN*sight*

The list of possible business opportunities is inexhaustible, and they are often driven by fads. The hottest fad a few years ago was for 900 telephone numbers. The investor would buy a few 900 telephone numbers and then place advertising to encourage callers. The money charged to callers would be earned by the investor after paying the promoter for the service. Many of these programs were shut down by enforcement cases brought by the Federal Trade Commission because of misrepresentations and promises by the promoters. More recently, the hot concept was selling yellow-page ads for Internet shopping malls. The Internet is likely to be a long-lasting fad.

The key concept underlying the business opportunity is that it enables the purchaser "to begin a business." Obviously, if you buy at wholesale a dozen boxes of gumballs, greeting cards, or snack foods for your own distribution, it is not a business opportunity. The gumballs seller offers nothing that will enable you to begin a business. There are no promises of training, coaching, or location assistance, and no one promises you a "territory" or assures you that you will make money with your "investment." In short, the product seller does not represent that you will be able to begin a business with the purchase of its product at wholesale.

The analysis changes when the seller of the product puts together a package of goods, information, and/or services designed to allow the buyer to begin a business of distributing goods or services. *Then* it has the look, touch, and feel of a business opportunity package.

The package also generally has a seductive selling angle that appeals to people looking to make some easy money. Business opportunity sellers often claim you can make substantial money by having fun, doing something that is simple and easy, or working only a couple of hours a week. Many hardworking couples pressed for money are looking for a way to bring in a little extra income, and are naturally interested in an inexpensive package that allows them to do that.

THE HARD SELL

The business opportunity sales effort usually goes further by touching one or more of the "big six" hot buttons embedded in the psyche of ambitious Americans. You'll recognize the hard-sell pitches here:

1. Spend more time with your family.
2. Tell the boss to take his job and shove it.
3. Work from home, drop the commute, and enjoy flexible hours.
4. Be your own boss, own your own business.
5. Enjoy income security; you could be laid off from your job.
6. This business has unlimited income generating potential if you are ambitious and willing to follow the program.

Americans are raised with strong cultural images of home and business ownership. Business ownership is seen—correctly—as the most common way to success and true wealth in this country. Business opportunity sellers will frequently make a hard sell by appealing to the myths and the dreams of their buyers. They may promise riches, or a simple business concept that "anyone can run," or a purchase price that can fit on a credit card. They make the dream of business ownership seem possible to the common man, both practically ("Even I can do this") and financially ("It's only a few thousand dollars. I'll just charge it to my VISA card").

If you pay by credit card and the seller disappoints you or does not deliver on promised deliveries, you may be able to object to your credit card company that you should not be required to pay the original charge. Check with your credit card issuers as to the ground rules for such an objection.

An effective business opportunity seller makes their program *sound* great: "It's simple, it's fun, even you can do it." In a sense they take on one of the great challenges in sales, the large impulse purchase. They make their package sound as if it is within the reach of everyone, not just the educated, experienced, or already well-off. Masters of closing techniques, they know how to impart a serious sense of urgency. Here are just a few of the claims you might hear: "There are only a few territories left." "I'm getting on a plane at 5:30 this afternoon and won't be returning to this area." "I brought only a few of these packages with me today, so the first ones in line will get them." "This computer/Internet/vending device is hot right now, but the competition will be closing in soon." "Can you afford another year of waiting for opportunity to hit you over the head?"

INsight

To resist the hard sell and various closing techniques, see them for what they are: sales tricks. Smile to yourself when you hear a closing pitch and compliment the seller on a "good one." Hold your ground and move at your own speed. If you appear to be a serious buyer, the seller will not let you go.

THE BUSINESS OPPORTUNITY MARKETPLACE

I have always thought of the business opportunity seller as the modern embodiment of the early American medicine man, that fast-talking peddler of various nostrums, potions, and cure-alls who traveled from town to town selling his folk remedies to unsuspecting people. Just as when the rascally protagonist in *The Music Man* sells the town on the wholesome image of a boys marching band, there is a sense in the business opportunity sales exchange that the buyer knows he is being sold a dream, and wants badly to believe in the promises being spun by the seller. Buying the business opportunity package becomes little more than a wistful affirmation of the buyer's American dream of business ownership.

SUMMARY NOTES

- A business opportunity package is designed to allow the buyer to be in business. It is self-contained and affordable.
- With most business opportunity programs there is no continuing relationship or support for the buyer, no control exercised by the seller, and there are no royalty fees.
- Watch out for the hard sell in the business opportunity arena.

ACTION PLAN

Sit down with a few business opportunity sellers and see what they have to offer and what it will cost. Take the concept to a few trusted friends and ask them what they think. If things look good, research the company and talk to as many current buyers as you can.

BUSINESS OPPORTUNITY REGULATION

*S*AM, *A STATE LEGISLATOR WHO IS A SENIOR MEMBER OF THE* *Commerce Committee, attended his committee's* *hearing on proposals to regulate business opportuni-* *ties in the state. Lobbyists for the direct selling companies* *like Avon skin care products and Amway products were* *saying that the bill could have a serious impact on their* *business if the definitions are written too broadly. Their* *businesses are generally not regulated by these laws any-* *way, they say. Where, Sam wondered, are the companies* *who would be directly affected by the business opportu-* *nity bill?*

This is a scenario that I have actually experienced. In the dozen or so state legislatures that I saw adopt business opportunity bills, no group or individual ever showed up to say, "Wait a minute, this legislation will regulate my business."

The lesson was not lost on me. These bills were not carefully designed through legislative give-and-take; nor were they designed so that compliance was efficient and easy. Just the opposite was true: this legislation was enacted as a rather crude club to be used by state authorities to chase out those they considered to be bad actors. The legislation was always in the posture of a registration law, giving the somewhat misleading impression that any company could comply by simply applying to the right state agency. This means state business opportunity laws represent the chilling conclusion that all business opportunity packages— at least those that meet the definitions in the statutes—are unacceptable in the eyes of the law.

Whether unacceptable or not, business opportunity sales are big business in the United States. Thousands of prepackaged programs are offered and sold to investors who fancy going into business for themselves.

NATIONAL REGULATION

During the 1970s and 1980s when the state business opportunity laws were proposed, the moving forces were exclusively enforcement authorities. Attorneys general had run into difficulties prosecuting flimflam artists who had taken business opportunity style investments from state residents and skipped town. It was—and still is—difficult to prove legal fraud. It was also difficult for enforcement agencies to move quickly enough to shut down a scam operation before investors had already been fleeced. The business opportunity laws were the answer to both problems. The statutes could be broadly drafted and could require presale registration. That means that the enforcement agency could simply check the list of registered companies and if a particular operation was not on it, take immediate action.

Over a period of about 25 years, 25 states and the Federal Trade Commission (FTC) adopted laws that impose a variety of requirements on companies and individuals who sell packages that qualify as "business opportunities." Some statutes call the concept "seller-assisted marketing plans." The FTC adopted a set of business opportunity regulations as part of its 1979 Franchise Rule basically requiring full presale disclosure, but it included a definition of a business opportunity venture that was so loose it reached only a fraction of the companies covered by the state laws. The FTC is currently considering splitting the Franchise Rule into two sections so that business opportunities will be separately regulated, with the scope of the definitions and compliance requirements rewritten.

THE ENFORCEMENT TOOL

The state laws require the seller to register its offering with the designated state agency and deliver a disclosure document to the prospective purchaser in advance of making a sale. When a seller registers the offering it is generally effective for a year. At the end of the registration term the company must renew the registration or it lapses and the company is no longer authorized to offer and sell business opportunities.

REGULATION BACKGROUND

The presale disclosure concept mirrors the requirements of franchise law, and indeed was designed to run parallel to the franchise requirements. As much sense as this might make to legislators, there is one huge difference between franchising and business opportunity sales: a business opportunity is essentially an impulse purchase. It is made in the heat of the moment, when the salesperson has inspired the buyer to believe that they can succeed, that the device or product is a guaranteed home run, and that the purchase can be placed on a credit card and will quickly pay for itself. This differs from a franchise, which is usually a larger investment; it takes more thought, time, and money.

An impulse business opportunity purchase does not lend itself to pre-sale disclosure and a two week cooling off period before the sale can be closed. Either the marketing people or the lawyers will be completely frustrated by efforts to comply with presale cooling off in an impulse purchase business. That's just fine with state regulators. They don't want consumers making heat-of-the-moment decisions to invest in something that may be vapor.

This tension is a principal factor in a startling fact: business opportunity sellers generally don't register under the state business opportunity laws. They usually ignore the laws, and hope they can duck the enforcement radar. Their reasoning goes like this: "If we are careful to make sure that all purchasers are happy, and that we return money to those who are not happy, the odds of our coming to the attention of the state attorney general are slim. And even if we do come to their attention, it will be 'no harm, no foul.'"

Some business opportunity sellers sell their programs for a price so low that the state business opportunity laws do not apply. Most states define a business opportunity as requiring a payment of $500 or more. Some states have a lower threshold than that.

Where does this leave the investor? Companies are confounded by a dysfunctional regulatory attempt that was not designed for compliance; disclosure is not uniformly required, the federal government has been ineffective in creating a national compliance standard, and there is widespread noncompliance by most companies. For the investor this has the effect of dramatically increasing the risks of loss when buying a business opportunity.

Take a closer look at the business opportunity laws. In the early 1970s the North Carolina legislature hammered out the first attempt at regulating business opportunities. At the time it was a new concept, and the regulators focused on the key problem: unfounded promises of profitability and assistance combined with a substantial purchase of goods or services. Since that time a couple dozen states and the FTC have adopted their own versions of the North Carolina formula.

The state statutory formula defines a business opportunity as a sale of goods and/or services that allows the purchaser to begin a business, and one in which the seller makes one of several representations to the buyer.

The following statements are the types of representations that constitute a business opportunity:

- "I will refund your money if you are dissatisfied in any way."
- "Don't worry about locations. I will help you find profitable locations for your whole string of vending machines."
- "We will buy back from you all of the product you produce."
- "This is a can't miss proposition. I guarantee you'll make money with this simple business."
- "I'll provide training so that you know as much as I do about the business. We'll lay out the whole marketing plan for you. It's already been done."

Each of these statements forms a part of the definition of a business opportunity. When one is delivered with a purchase of $500 or more, it's a business opportunity.

The last statement promises the buyer a "marketing plan." This huge, gaping concept pulls in almost every distribution program in which the seller provides any advice or training to the buyer in conjunction with the sale. It is often impossible for a distribution company to avoid this broad definition of a marketing plan. If the seller provides promotional literature, brochures, pamphlets, or advertising materials, that's a marketing plan. If they provide a training course to the buyer regarding the promotion, operation, or management of the package, that's a marketing plan, too. If they provide operational, managerial, technical, or financial guidelines or assistance, they've met the definition.

COMPLIANCE

If a company meets the definition and is unavoidably selling a business opportunity package, what is the consequence? Most of the business opportunity laws require that the seller meet the same basic regulatory requirements as a franchisor: (1) register the offering with state officials (with a yearly renewal requirement), and (2) provide a presale disclosure document to the buyer. The period of the required disclosure before the sale varies from one state to the next. The FTC time period is ten business days. The FTC disclosure timing preempts shorter periods under state law, although it is possible that the business opportunity is not covered by the FTC Rule and so will have a shorter period before the sale in some states.

If a company does take steps to comply with the state law, it will prepare a brief disclosure statement that can be considerably shorter than a franchise disclosure statement. It may be no more than four or five pages in length. That document will be on file with the appropriate state authority. A phone call to the right agency will tell you if the company is registered. If you think a company should be registered and it is not, ask why not. There may or may not be a good answer to the question (it may truly not meet the definition). I have heard several nonsense answers. My personal favorite is, "We're a corporation so it is not required of us." Such wonderful balderdash! If you think you are being fed a line of nonsense, move on down the line. If you are feeling public spirited, you can contact the attorney general and report your experience.

A business opportunity disclosure statement will deliver the basic information about the program, but it is often short on the information you really need to know, like names, addresses, and phone numbers of current owners. Use the disclosure as your research starting point only.

The laws put significant buyer protections in place. Depending on the state, compliance may mean that the seller is required to establish a bond or trust account that can be used to pay damages to injured buyers. A seller who promises a later delivery of goods may be required to set up an escrow account and place a portion of the purchase price in that account until the delivery is made. These financial safeguards help

BUSINESS OPPORTUNITY REGULATION STATES

The following 25 states now specifically regulate business opportunity sales. Check with consumer protection agencies—often a part of the attorney general's office—in your state.

Alabama	Louisiana	Oklahoma
California	Maine	South Carolina
Connecticut	Maryland	South Dakota
Florida	Michigan	Texas
Georgia	Minnesota	Utah
Illinois	Nebraska	Virginia
Indiana	New Hampshire	Washington
Iowa	North Carolina	
Kentucky	Ohio	

buyers who lose money in a business opportunity venture. The laws also create a private right to sue the seller if a buyer is damaged, and may provide for punitive damages or the award of attorney fees.

SUMMARY NOTES

- Business opportunity laws were adopted to give state regulators an enforcement tool to use against flimflam artists.
- Legal compliance with disclosure and registration is difficult; many companies simply don't comply. Compliance requires state registration and disclosure delivery.
- As many as 25 states and the FTC regulate business opportunity sales.

ACTION PLAN

Research a business opportunity company that you find interesting: call the Better Business Bureau, call your state consumer protection agencies, visit the FTC Web site (www.ftc.gov), and chase down any questions you have until you are satisfied that you have a clear picture of the company.

MAKE SURE YOU ARE WELL SUITED TO OWN A BUSINESS OPPORTUNITY

*R*OB SAW AN ADVERTISEMENT FOR A BUSINESS OPPORTUNITY *package. It promised that any buyer of typical intelligence could make up to $2,000 a week with minimal part-time effort. It sounded good to Rob; he had a job he liked, but he wanted to make more money. If the business took off, he thought, he might quit the job (it wasn't THAT good) and work the business opportunity full time. Would it be worth the $3,500 investment?*

Like Rob, you may wonder if you are well suited to buy a business opportunity. That depends largely on the size of the investment, and the level of involvement that the business requires. A business opportunity package that sells for $1,500 and is designed for you to work it a couple of hours a week doesn't need much introspection or planning. Many such business opportunities give you a chance to dip your big toe in the water without plunging into the deep end of the business pool with a total immersion franchise. If it costs $50,000 however, and replaces your regular job, you may want to think twice.

Actually, the key question most business opportunity buyers need to ask is *not* "Am I well suited to the business?" but "Can I afford to lose the entire investment?" I have seen hundreds of people buy into fad business opportunities using groaning credit cards, while I knew with certainty that no more than 1 percent of these buyers will ever take the shrink-wrapped package down from the shelf and read it, let alone put it into action. It is akin to seeing someone buy a packed parachute when they have no intention of jumping out of a plane. It's there "just in case." To some people owning the parachute is a comforting end in itself. It says, "I am serious enough about possibly jumping out of a plane that I own this here parachute." Or, "I am covered if I am ever pushed out of a plane."

Hmmm.

The best way to think of a business opportunity is not as a parachute for difficult times, but as a tool. It is not a motivator or a security blanket, but can be a rational means to a meaningful end.

INsight

Most business opportunity packages are self-contained sales positions, and it is useful to think of them that way. Too many business opportunity sales representatives will play down the sales aspect of their programs. Whether you are distributing greetings cards on display racks, women's hose, or advertising for Internet directories, you will be selling.

When boiled down, virtually every business opportunity is an independent sales position in which you sell a product or service as best as you can, on your own. In many cases you buy an inventory of products and resell them, or receive "training" in how to promote and provide a service using a device or specialized equipment.

QUESTIONS TO ASK ABOUT THE BUSINESS OPPORTUNITY AND ABOUT YOU

To determine whether a business opportunity is right for you, try asking yourself the following questions:

Can I Sell?

If the business opportunitiy is a sales position, this is the first and most important question to ask. If you have never held a real sales position and don't know the answer to that question, then this may be your introduction to the concept of selling.

Never be so naïve as to buy the business opportunity seller's line that this product or service "will sell itself." The typical seller is excited and speaks with unflinching enthusiasm for the product or service. If they succeed in convincing you that it is a good idea, it will be easy for you to leap to the conclusion that others will be as quickly sold on it as you are. Naturally you assume that it will virtually sell itself. In fact, selling takes hard work and considerable skill. Good salespeople tend to have outgoing personalities who like talking to people. They are upbeat, can quickly connect with their customers, but not take rejection personally. They have a natural enthusiasm for their products and can convey that enthusiasm with ease. Do you see yourself in this picture?

Is this Business Opportunity Package a Complete Tool?

Is the product or service a good one, and most importantly, is there a market for it? Be objective about your own enthusiasm and do some market research. Meet with friends and people you know in business. Show them the product and ask if it is something they would be interested in buying and if so, how much they would be willing to spend for it. Stop people on the street, tell them you are doing market research, and show them the product. Note their reactions and comments. If the product is to be placed in a retail location, go talk to some retailers about their level of interest.

For instance, if you are evaluating a purchase of ten tabletop vending machines that allow customers to measure the level of alcohol on their breath, you had better know about the bar business. Will a bar owner allow you to place one of these devices in their establishment? Or will they tell you that such devices don't work, customers don't like or use them, and liability is a concern if a machine gives a customer an erroneous passing mark and then an accident occurs and it is determined that the customer had blood alcohol levels well above legal limits? If the owner likes the machine, where will it be placed? On the bar or in a dark corner by the restrooms? Will you have to carry insurance on the machine in case it is damaged by frustrated and inebriated customers? Will the bar owner demand a portion of the revenues generated by the machine, and if so, what portion? If the machine breaks, will you fix or replace it?

The questions go on and on, and in my experience the most important and practical ones are too often glossed over in the business opportunity sales presentation. Too many business opportunity packages are sold to buyers who do not know anything about the business or the marketplace into which they will be selling. Consequently, the buyer does not ask the right questions but simply goes along with the sales pitch. If you are seriously considering buying something like the bar vending machines, ask yourself this question: Would a bar owner or a regional distributor of bar equipment with 20 years experience buy this string of ten alcohol breath machines? Or would they both split a side laughing at the concept?

Can I Work on My Own?

Expect to be completely on your own while selling products or services through your business opportunity. Unlike a business franchise, a business opportunity package is a one-time purchase with no continuing relationship or support.

Are you a self-starter? Do you mind working on your own or prefer the company of partners, co-workers, or even the hand-holding of a franchisor? If you don't need support to make the business go—that is if you are a dyed-in-the-wool entrepreneur—then you have the temperament to find success as a business opportunity package owner.

Do I Mind Making Sales Calls on Friends and Family?

All purchasers of new sales-based businesses must confront this question. It is especially pressing if you are involved in a multilevel marketing program like Mary Kay cosmetics or Amway. The key here is to make sure you have confidence in the product or service you are selling. One budding multilevel entrepreneur reported signing up his mother-in-law for a long-distance service package that succeeded only in completely disabling Mom's telephone service for three weeks. Not a pretty sight.

Am I a Good Negotiator?

This is an essential strength for anyone going into business. So much depends on your ability to negotiate the best price for the services and products you buy, as well as those you will sell. Negotiation makes business go 'round. Unlike the consumer purchasing world, the business world runs on individually negotiated transactions. If you do not understand this fact you will be small-business roadkill. Almost all small businesses operate on razor-thin margins and do not have much revenue left over after their expenses are paid. The only way to succeed is to protect the margins: keep expenses to a reasonable minimum and selling prices sufficiently high to cover your costs. In order to pull that off, you must be prepared to negotiate whenever you can.

Why not start with the terms on which you purchase the business opportunity package? If it is offered for $2,100, and you are concerned about the company's ability to deliver on its promises, propose to the seller that a portion of the fee be deferred. You might suggest that you are prepared to pay the full purchase price in three installments of $700, with the first paid on purchase, and the balance over some specified period of time. Maybe you could key the deferred payments to the scheduled delivery dates of inventory. Think creatively. Offer to pay a discounted $1,800 up front, not on your credit card but by a certified check.

You may be shot down, but then again you may save a few hundred dollars. Much depends on just how anxious the seller is to move his packages, and the margin he has built into his asking price.

Be creative and be bold. It's the key to success as a small business owner.

SUMMARY NOTES

- Can you afford to lose your entire investment in a business opportunity?
- Ask some tough questions about the package: Is it complete? Is there a market for the product?
- Buy a business opportunity for the right reason, as a tool in your business plans.
- Look to your own skills: Do you like to work on your own? Do you like to sell? Are you a negotiator?

ACTION PLAN

Explore your potential as a salesperson. Head to the library and find books on business sales. Practice a basic sales pitch, first in front of the mirror, then with a trusted family member or friend. Here's a great study idea: go shopping for a car, new or used, and watch the sales pitch made to you. Is it effective, pleasant, and persuasive? Does the salesperson instill trust in his organization and his products?

PART III

THE GREAT AMERICAN BUSINESS FORMAT FRANCHISE

UNDERSTANDING THE FRANCHISE CONCEPT

*P*AUL HAD ALWAYS WANTED TO OWN HIS OWN BUSINESS, BUT THE *opportunity had just never presented itself. On a fishing trip to Minnesota he came across a business concept that he could not get out of his mind. It was new and fresh, and he thought it had a huge market potential. He wanted to get in on the business somehow and learned it was being offered as a new franchise program. This might mean he could bring the concept to his hometown and open a sensational business. He had never considered a franchise. Where should he start?*

INDEPENDENT OWNERSHIP

Start at the beginning, a business format franchise is a long-term business relationship in which the purchaser (the "franchisee") is granted the right to operate a business under the trademark of an established business owner (the "franchisor") and use its business techniques. This franchise relationship gives the franchisee the right to start up a business concept that the franchisor has already invented and perfected, using an established trademark and a comprehensive set of operating techniques. (We will discuss the legal definition of a franchise in Chapter 8.)

Once licensed to use the franchisor's trademark and business system, the franchisee has the right to set up a business—usually under the franchisor's close scrutiny—that looks and operates *exactly* like other franchises in the franchise network. The magic in this formula—the simple fact that drives the success of the entire concept of business franchising—is that *the franchise owner remains an independent businessperson.* A franchisee is never an employee and is subject only to the limited control exercised by the franchisor under the franchise agreement. Independence means that if the franchisee is very successful in operating the business, they will reap the financial rewards. And the rewards can be substantial: franchising has created an untold number of millionaires (think McDonald's and Holiday Inn). Of course, the converse also remains true: if the franchised business is not successful, the franchisee absorbs the loss.

THE BUSINESS OF FRANCHISING

Contrary to the impression conveyed nightly by the business press, it is small business ownership, not big business, that is the bedrock strength of the American economy. Franchising gives the individual investor the opportunity to own their own small business without having to go it alone or invent and perfect a profitable retail concept that is, statistically at least, doomed to failure.

The franchise relationship we describe here has been adopted by hundreds of successful business programs, many of which are familiar cultural icons: McDonald's, Jiffy Lube, Jani King, Holiday Inn, Dairy Queen, Quality Inn, Burger King, Subway, Midas Muffler, and 7-11 stores. Many American towns have strip malls and mile-long commercial streets that are dominated by such franchised businesses.

While quick-service restaurants may be some of the best known franchises, the franchise concept has actually been applied in more than 50 different industry categories. These include everything from cellular telephone networks and formalwear rental businesses, to automobile dent removal and paper shredding businesses.

Are gas station dealers and automobile dealers part of business franchising? Yes and no. Most systems are made up of independent dealers licensed to operate under a particular company's trademark and are said to own "product franchises," but they generally do not pay the franchise fees described here. The traditional practice in these industries is for dealers to buy product from the manufacturer at wholesale and sell it through their dealerships at retail. In contrast, the McDonald's restaurant franchisee does not buy any product from the franchisor—not even one sesame seed. Supplies are bought exclusively from third-party suppliers approved by the company. Ray Kroc, the legendary founder of the McDonald's system, did not want any buyer/seller tension to creep into his relationship with franchise owners.

Franchising by itself is not an "industry," but a form of distribution. The franchisor is distributing product and services through licensed franchisees. This is important because two businesses may be franchised, say a convenience store and a hotel, but have absolutely nothing else in common.

In the past several years there has also been an explosive growth in international franchising. The McDonald's trademark has become nothing short of a symbol of American culture, the restaurant's golden arches established now in more than 120 countries.

THE FRANCHISEE VIEW

Consider three important measures of a franchise system from the franchisee point of view: independence, training, and money dynamics.

Independent Ownership

This concept energizes franchising because of the motivation, commitment, and drive of an on-site owner. An employee manager working on an hourly wage is usually not motivated to work as hard or as long as an owner. It's that simple: an employee is involved; an owner is committed. It is the lesson taught when a pig and a chicken form a partnership to produce a ham and egg sandwich, the chicken is "involved," but the pig is *committed*.

Training Says It All

Training and support are keys to a strong business franchise. A well-established franchisor has something valuable to impart to the franchisee: *know-how*. It's one thing to perfect a business concept; it is quite another to transfer the essence of that concept to someone who knows nothing about the business and enable them to find success.

IN*sight*

Among franchisors the phrase "fast food" is discouraged. As commonly used,
it has become a pejorative comment on the quality of the food. Preferred,
more politically correct expressions in franchise circles include
"quick service" food and "quality service" restaurants.
I like "quick cuisine."

The strongest and best franchise programs are those able to convey know-how through rigorous training. The country's leading fresh-baked whole wheat bread franchisor, Great Harvest Bread Co., requires that new franchisees spend one week in classroom training at its Montana headquarters and another two weeks doing hands-on training in an existing franchised bakery in their system. Additional in-store training takes place when the franchisee opens for business.

HOW THE MONEY WORKS

How does the money work in a franchise relationship? While there are no hard and fast rules, the franchisee generally pays the franchisor three ways: the initial franchise fee, royalties, and advertising contributions.

The *initial franchise fee* is a lump sum paid when the contract is signed. This payment can range from a few thousand dollars to as high as $50,000 or more. A typical initial franchise fee for a restaurant franchise is in the $20,000 to $30,000 range. This fee generally covers the franchisor's cost of recruiting franchisees and of initial services, like site location and training.

The franchisee also pays the franchisor a continuing *royalty fee*. This is usually calculated as a percentage of the business's gross sales, somewhere in the range of 3 to 8 percent. It is important to understand the significance of the royalty fee being calculated on gross sales rather than on a net figure or a flat fee basis, such as $500 per month. Calculating the royalty on gross sales means that the percentage is measured on every dollar that comes in the door. Gross sales are those that are made by the business before any expenses, salaries, rent, or other overhead is paid. They have nothing to do with the profitability of the business or with the net income that the owner might take home. Naturally, the franchisor wants to see the gross sales of the franchise maximized, since this increases the level of royalties paid. However, the franchisee, like any business owner, wants to maximize *profitability*. The franchisor does not have a direct interest in seeing that the business is run efficiently or profitably. The cold reality is that the franchisor will be paid the royalty whether or not the business is profitable for the franchisee.

The royalty fee is similar to a rent calculation. Your commercial land-lord cares little whether your operation is profitable; however if the rent is partly calculated on gross sales, he cares a lot that the gross sales fig-ures are high. Both franchisor and landlord leave the task of making the business profitable entirely to the franchisee. A franchisee may have annual sales of $500,000 and pay the franchisor $25,000 in royalties (5 percent of gross sales), but still be losing money. Obviously, the fran-chisor wants to see every franchisee running a profitable business because healthy, profitable franchisees stay in business and keep paying royalties, but the franchisee is the only business player in this game with a direct interest in *profitability*.

Finally, most franchisees pay *advertising fund contributions*. Many franchisors organize franchise owners in a particular market or region and have them pool their advertising money for coordinated expendi-tures that benefit all stores operating under the system trademarks. This fee is usually within a range of 1 to 4 percent of gross sales.

If those are all of the fees paid to the franchisor, the rest of the busi-ness expenses must be assumed by the franchise owner, as with any other form of business. At the same time, the revenues from the business belong to the franchisee.

In business terms, then, a franchise is a form of joint venture, with the neophyte paying the experienced company for the right to conduct a business using all the techniques that made the experienced company successful. The franchisor has its arm around the shoulders of the fran-chisee, training and assisting, and showing exactly how to run the busi-ness. A good franchisor is a patient mentor, a relentless teacher, and a demanding partner.

With such a robust market of franchisors, you can expect to find brand new sparkling programs, fading giants, troubled systems with rebellious franchise owners, systems on the way up, and systems crumbling under the weight of competition.

Be on the lookout for fad franchises that sound snazzy but probably won't be around long enough for you to get any return on your investment. My all-time favorite is the freestanding bungee-jump tower franchise of a few years ago; a close second is the corrugated cardboard coffins dealerships spotted at a franchise trade show in the late 1980s. Other fads might include laser tag games, bagel stores, and yogurt shops. Also look out for businesses that may be eclipsed by fundamental changes in equipment or the marketplace. How would you like to have a franchise for the best typewriter repair shop in town? The Internet is profoundly changing lots of businesses, such as travel agencies. Don't get stuck with a buggy-whip franchise. So before you invest in such a company, you owe it to yourself to do the research, just as you would before buying stock in a publicly traded corporation.

The underlying message here should be clear: you can get hurt financially if you invest in the wrong franchise.

THE ALL-AMERICAN HARD SELL

One feature of a robust franchise marketplace is that franchisors are under extreme pressure to make the franchise sale. They have invested heavily in their program (it takes a chunk of change to pull together the business organization and meet the legal requirements), and the sales process itself is difficult and time consuming. The cost of the sale (representative's salary, trade show costs, advertising, promotional materials, etc.) can also be substantial. The result is often the all-American hard sell: sales representatives pressing too hard to move a vaguely interested prospect to make a commitment, selling a franchise to anyone with a heartbeat, and making untenable promises or inappropriate representations about the financial potential of the business. Many franchisor sales specialists will employ crude closing techniques that would make a used car salesman proud.

INsight

Many franchise sales representatives are paid a large portion of their salary on commission, and will sometimes bring an overenthusiasm to their work that gets them in trouble with their employers, and sometimes with consumer protection agencies or franchise regulators.

Never allow yourself to be stampeded into making a franchise investment decision because of urgencies created by the sales representative. "Buy today before the price increase," "Territories are going fast. Get in on this or the prime markets will be taken," and "We only have a couple territories left," are just some of the claims you might hear. In all likelihood, these statements are entirely false. If you could see behind the curtain, you would understand that the salesman is scrambling to make his sales numbers, probably paid on straight commission, and having a devil of a time closing on his leads. He wants to close you on *his* schedule, not yours.

Your best defense is to anticipate this hard sell and use it to your advantage. Learn to hear and appreciate a closing technique for what it is—a salesperson working hard to move you to commitment. Know that many franchise organizations would love to have you buy into their business concept, but in front of the curtain are cool about their eagerness. The better companies want to make sure that there is a great match between their concept and their franchisees, and want to spend time exploring that match with a prospective investor. Ask them what qualifications they look for in a franchisee and what strengths among franchisees have lead to success in their business. By listening closely during the sales process, you will learn a lot about the business of franchising.

Here is a little-known secret in franchising: the buyer has an enormous amount of control and power in the sales process. Many franchisors make buyers feel unworthy or poorly qualified to own and operate the franchise. They portray themselves as powerful trademark owners who control all aspects of their business, and they require detailed information in order for prospects to qualify for the right to buy a franchise. However, the prospective franchisee actually has the greater power since they can choose to invest or move on to the next opportunity. Experienced franchisors are aware of this; but you wouldn't know it from the noise surrounding most franchise sales.

The business of franchising is not slow, sedate, and welcoming. It is fast, exciting, a hard sell, and sometimes intimidating to the uninitiated. But read on. By the time you finish this book, you won't qualify as uninitiated anymore.

SUMMARY NOTES

- A business format franchise is a continuing relationship in which the franchisee is granted rights to operate under the trademark, business format, and techniques owned by the franchisor.
- As a franchisee you are an independent business owner, never an employee. That includes risk and reward, success and failure.
- Franchisors like to say that in a franchise you are in business for yourself, not by yourself.
- Training is one key to a successful franchise program.
- Initial franchise fees, royalties, and advertising fees define your money relationship with the franchisor.

- Franchising represents a huge marketplace, so it takes some research to find a solid program.

ACTION PLAN

Identify as many franchises in your immediate market as you can, and list them. Ask the managers if the business is a franchise and where you can learn more about the program. Look up the businesses on the Internet and send away for franchise information of those business concepts you like.

7

BUYING MULTIPLE FRANCHISE RIGHTS

*G*EORGE HAS THE HIGHEST CAREER AMBITIONS OF ANYONE IN
*his family. He longs for a life of wealth and is deter-
mined to get there. Business ownership appeals to
him, and he understands that most millionaires in the
U.S. own their own businesses. He is interested in buying a
franchised business but is already looking down the road
to his second, fifth, and tenth businesses. George never has
done anything on a small scale.*

Most investors like George and many franchise owners
understand the real path to substantial personal wealth is
ownership of multiple retail businesses. Many ultrasuccess-
ful franchisees establish a profitable franchised operation

and then o on to develop or buy a dozen other franchised businesses. Before they know it, they have built an empire.

Multiple franchise development is a challenging part of the franchising business and varies from one company to the next. Is it possible to purchase the right to develop an entire state or region of the country? Do you need to be a subfranchisor or master franchisee for a region, or is there another way? What legal rights are granted for multiple franchise ownership? What if the franchise owner wants to purchase only two or three additional units?

TYPES OF MULTI-UNIT FRANCHISE PROGRAMS

Start with a look at some of the basic concepts of multiple franchising.

Multiple Unit Ownership

This is when the same individual is granted franchise rights at more than one location. Most franchisors encourage multiple unit ownership once a franchisee shows they are capable of operating a successful business. Everybody wins under this arrangement. The franchisee expands their business one step at a time, as their resources grow. The franchisor enhances its relationship with successful franchise owners, rewarding those that prove themselves successful. The franchisor does not have the costs and risks associated with recruiting a new franchisee into the system. No special legal rights are created for multiple unit ownership. The franchisor simply grants standard unit franchise rights for newly identified locations or markets. Some companies will grant a right of first refusal, which says essentially, "We will give you the first shot at another franchise in this market if we want to grant one." Once George has established one restaurant, he requests the rights to another across town, and the franchisor decides to grant him a unit franchise agreement exactly like his first franchise. A year later he may want to go for a third.

Area Franchise

Here the franchisor grants the franchisee, through a contract usually referred to as a development agreement, the right to develop a specified number of franchised units in a given territory. The development agreement details the time frame in which the units must be developed and opened for business, development quotas, the geographic area in which the franchisee has rights, and the fee obligations that apply. This type of development agreement is essentially an option agreement with a development schedule; it grants the developer option rights to enter into contracts in the future.

Master Franchise

With a master franchise agreement the franchisor grants to a franchisee in its system the limited right to recruit new franchisees and to provide specified field support services to franchisees in a given area. In exchange, the master franchisee receives a commission on franchise sales made and a percentage of the royalty revenues generated among the franchisees it serves. George's franchisor appoints him to serve as a master franchisee in Texas. He runs advertising to generate interested investors in Texas and meets with all prospects who respond. Serious, qualified investors are sent to the franchisor's headquarters where the sale is closed. George has a regular schedule for visiting all 19 Texas franchises twice a year and runs three regional meetings each year. In return, George receives 35 percent of the initial franchise fees of sales made through his efforts and 25 percent of all royalties paid by Texas franchisees.

Subfranchising

Under a subfranchising arrangement the franchisor grants to another entity (a subfranchisor) the right to enter into unit franchise agreements with subfranchisees in a specified area. The franchisor usually dictates

Most franchisors have explored concepts of multiple unit franchising and have settled on their own approach. Ask the sales representative what the company has done in the past and what it offers now. You may find that a development agreement is included in the company's unit offering Uniform Franchise Offering Circular (UFOC). Other companies may have a separate UFOC for their multiple unit offering.

the terms on which unit franchises are granted. As a subfranchisor, George has near complete autonomy in the franchise sales process. He actually grants franchises, provides training and field support, and has the right to collect royalties and advertising contributions. George must pay to the franchisor 45 percent of all franchise revenue.

The most common of these types of multiple-unit programs is the area franchise. If an investor wants to secure the right to develop a large number of franchises in a favorite market, they should consider negotiating for a development agreement. A development agreement has the advantage of being relatively straightforward conceptually. It balances the aggression of the large developer with the franchisor's need to make sure that a designated market is fully developed in a timely manner.

The least common type of multiple-unit program is subfranchising. True subfranchising is relatively rare in the world of franchising. Wendy's Old Fashioned Hamburger® restaurants and Century 21® real estate franchise programs are two of the best-known systems to use subfranchising relationships.

PROTECTING YOUR DEVELOPMENT INVESTMENT

In order to balance these interests and risks financially, the developer usually pays upfront a substantial portion of the initial franchise fees of the units to be developed. Look at a quick example. Our ambitious George signs a development agreement and receives the right to open six restaurants in Salt Lake City over ten years. He pays a non-refundable, upfront development fee of $60,000, which represents half of the $20,000 per store initial franchise fee for the six units. The development agreement promises that George will have exclusive rights to develop Salt Lake City for the next decade. He signs six standard unit franchise agreements within his development period and achieves his financial ambition. If George defaults under the development agreement and slips off the development schedule agreed upon, he may forfeit the unallocated portion of the upfront $60,000.

Clearly, multiple franchise development occurs at the higher financial end of franchising. It can be extremely expensive to secure the rights to multiple franchises, and the legal rights granted can be quite complicated.

If you are presented with an opportunity to purchase the rights to multiple franchises, be sure to take the program to your attorney for a detailed review of your rights and obligations. Developers, especially those who are inexperienced in the business being franchised or who are not well capitalized, can put a significant investment at risk by signing onto an aggressive development schedule. When negotiating the terms of development, it is vital that the build-out schedule is reasonable and that the exchange of fees is properly weighted for the risks being taken by both sides.

SUMMARY NOTES

- There are several ways that multiple-franchise rights are granted.
- Development fees may be paid upfront, so it is important to protect the investment by carefully negotiating your legal rights.

ACTION PLAN

Read a development contract for a complete understanding of its dynamics. Sketch out a business plan and projection of the money that might be required to develop an entire market.

FRANCHISE
SALES REGULATION

*J*IM THOUGHT HE WAS BEING HUSTLED. THE FRANCHISOR HAD
*not delivered any information about its program, and
he was being pressured to sign a 40-page contract by
the end of the week before it was offered to "the next person in line for the territory." It didn't feel right. Jim wondered "Isn't there a body of franchise law that protects the
little guy?"*

Given the early franchise success of companies like
Holiday Inn and McDonald's and the sizzle that became
associated with anything franchised ("Get in now, this is the
next McDonald's!"), problems in the marketplace were perhaps inevitable.

In the 1970s a number of fraudulent operators sold empty franchise opportunities that were all sizzle and no steak. Many people lost money investing in "can't lose" franchise propositions, and their shocking stories were told in the press. It wasn't long before state and federal regulators moved in. A dozen states and the FTC defined the franchise business concept in statutes and imposed a strict set of rules for franchising, based in large part on state and federal securities regulation. The rules are designed to counter the tendency in franchising to overhype the opportunity and to provide the prospective franchisee investor with key information on which to base a purchase decision. A number of states have also adopted regulations designed to protect franchise owners from the arbitrary termination of their rights.

The franchise laws are similar in many ways to the business opportunity laws discussed in earlier chapters and were adopted at about the same time. Both sets of laws require that the seller register the offering with state authorities and provide presale disclosure of material information to prospective investors. The similarities end there. The two business concepts are conceptually very different, and the disclosure document for franchising is far more extensive than the disclosure required for business opportunities.

Franchise regulation has a huge influence on how franchising is practiced. The following is a discussion of these rules of the franchise road.

HOW THE LAW DEFINES A FRANCHISE

How is a franchise defined under franchise laws? Ready for a little law school action? The law regulates a franchise transaction when three distinct elements are present:

1. The franchisor licenses the right to use its trademark in the operation of the business;

2. The franchisor prescribes in substantial part a marketing plan or provides significant assistance or control over the franchisee's business (some state definitions look for a "community of interest" between the franchisor and the franchisee); and

3. The franchisee is required to pay, directly or indirectly, a fee for the right to participate in the franchise program.

If one of these elements is missing, whatever the business transaction is, it is not regulated as a business franchise. In many circumstances the investment is then regulated as that close cousin, the "business opportunity."

INsight

As a prospective franchisee, you should have little concern about complying with the franchise investment laws. They impose no obligations on you. But recognizing a franchise when you see one could be an important asset in protecting yourself. If you see a franchise but someone tells you it is not one, ask why not, and listen carefully! You may want to share your notes with your attorney or the enforcement authorities in your state.

It is quite possible to invest in a business program that enables you to start a business that is not a franchise. There are dozens and dozens of such programs available. You can spend a couple thousand dollars and receive a package of materials designed to teach you how to make money with a new business application of your computer. You are not granted the right to use a trademark, and you are expected to operate under your own name. It may be a business opportunity, but it is not a franchise.

THE CONSEQUENCES OF BEING A FRANCHISE

What if a transaction meets the franchise definition? Then there are three consequences:

Presale Disclosure Must Be Delivered

Under the FTC's Trade Regulation Rule on Franchising, if a franchise is offered anywhere in the United States, a franchisor must deliver a disclosure document to a prospective franchisee, using either the FTC's format or the Uniform Franchise Offering Circular (UFOC) format. (The Uniform Franchise Offering Circular is explained in Chapter 13.) The franchisor does not have to register or file anything with the FTC; complying with the disclosure requirements satisfies the requirements of the federal rule.

When must the UFOC be delivered to the prospective franchisee? Either (1) at the first face-to-face personal meeting for the purpose of discussing the franchise sale, or (2) at least ten business days before money is paid for the franchise or a binding franchise agreement is signed by the franchisee, whichever comes first. That means that the

> Talking to a franchisor representative at a trade show exhibitor's booth is not considered to be a "first personal meeting" that would trigger disclosure obligations, even though it is "face to face." The disclosure obligation will trigger if the meeting is a detailed, extended discussion about the franchise opportunity.

franchisor is not required by law to deliver a UFOC until fairly far along in the sales process. As you will see in Chapter 13, the UFOC is a gold mine of information for the franchise investor. Ask for one early; it will help you evaluate the offering.

The Offering Must Comply with State Law

Fourteen states (see the state chart list on the next page) require franchisors to file or register with the state officials prior to any offering activity taking place. The franchisor will submit its UFOC, adapted to meet the particular requirements of each state, along with an application form and the appropriate fees. State franchise examiners review the disclosure document to assure that it is complete. They do not determine if the offer is reasonable or exercise any judgment regarding whether it is a good deal, or fair. They only make sure that the franchisor has complied with the UFOC guidelines.

When approved, the franchisor is authorized to sell franchises and must renew the registration at the end of the registration period. Some states will grant a registration period of a full calendar year; others such as California and Hawaii will automatically end the registration period a certain number of days after the end of the franchisor's fiscal year. That means a company with a fiscal year ending on December 31 remains registered in Hawaii until February 28 and in California until April 20.

Relationship Laws May Apply

A transaction meeting the franchise definition may also fall under the protections of the various state franchise relationship laws. These generally prohibit termination and non-renewal of a franchise in the absence of "good cause." (See our discussion of the relationship laws in Chapter 19.)

So what does this mean for investors? Franchise investors receive a generous amount of valuable information in the disclosure document. If the franchisee is in 1 of the 14 registration states, it means that the franchisor has gone through the process of document review by state examiners and achieved registration, clearing an important hurdle in the life of a franchisor. It is not easy to become registered in these states, although some are tougher than others.

Registration is no guarantee for the investor, of course. It does not tell you anything about the company, and it is not a qualifier in any sense. It simply means that the company has taken an important step to comply with the law. It has filed its offering on the public record in that state and will remain under the annual scrutiny of the state officials.

If you live in one of the registration states, you should plan to call the appropriate agency (see appendix B) and confirm that the company is currently registered to offer and sell franchises.

FRANCHISE REGISTRATION STATES

California	Michigan	South Dakota
Hawaii	Minnesota	Virginia
Illinois	New York	Washington
Indiana	North Dakota	Wisconsin
Maryland	Rhode Island	

SUMMARY NOTES

- If a business meets the legal definition of a franchise, it will be regulated as a franchise.
- The consequences of meeting the franchise definition include disclosure, registration in a number of states, and possible application of relationship laws.
- Registration under a state law is no guarantee of anything.

ACTION PLAN

Call the appropriate agencies to find out how franchising is regulated in your state. Keep addresses and phone numbers for key state officials on file so you can contact them later with specific questions.

MAKE SURE YOU ARE WELL SUITED TO BE A FRANCHISEE

*B*ILL WAS EAGER TO GET INTO A GOOD BUSINESS AND JUMPED AT *the chance to buy an established one in his home town when he heard it was up for sale. It was a holiday ham and sandwich shop, and Bill soon learned it was also franchised. This meant every aspect of the operation—from the cases used to display product to the uniforms worn by the counter staff—was dictated by the terms of an operating manual. He had always wanted to own a business in which he could express his own creativity and off-beat sense of humor. Looking at the detailed operational requirements, he now wondered whether he was cut out to be a franchisee.*

IS A FRANCHISE FOR EVERYONE?

Clearly, owning a franchise is not for everyone. A capable person in the wrong program is not likely to stay happy for very long. Buying into a franchise is especially risky since the investment can involve your life's savings and a long-term legal commitment.

Fiercely independent entrepreneurs are rarely happy in the franchise harness. If you are interested in running and designing *every* aspect of the operation, think twice before you buy that franchise. You might actually be better off with your own independent business. Most franchising programs impose a strict regimen on franchise owners, dictating everything from how to greet customers to how to prepare and present the product or service, and many people find the restrictions far too confining. They might be better off choosing a business opportunity program which offers more independence.

If you have been a secure employee of a large corporation for a long time, the jolt of small business ownership can be difficult. A franchise owner has to put themselves completely into the daily operation of the business; small business owners do not delegate. They do *whatever needs to be done*. Remember the old line: you can always identify the owner of a small business—they are the one sweeping up after six o'clock.

Nevertheless, there are many downsized middle managers bringing a wealth of business savvy to the franchise market. They are at that stage in their careers where they have some capital to invest, are not interested in inventing a new (and risky) business concept, and yet are attracted to the dream of self-employment. For them, franchising may be the ticket.

QUESTIONS TO CONSIDER

A careful approach to deciding whether or not owning a franchise is for you starts with a self-examination and a brief planning exercise. Consider the following key questions:

1. *Are you motivated to invest the time and energy—not to mention money—necessary for small business ownership?* The first year of business can be especially trying; the time required to get a business up and running—even a sophisticated franchise—is intimidating. Your days of punching and watching the clock will be long gone. Small business ownership requires a sea change in your mental attitudes toward work, and a new level of dedication and perseverance.

2. *Is your family behind you?* Many businesses are designed for total family involvement. Even if you invest in one that is not, you cannot commit the time and energy needed without the full support of every member of your family. Have you discussed it in detail with them? Your spouse may be supportive but skeptical (which is healthy). Involve them in the decision-making process and listen to all their doubts or concerns. Try to help your kids understand that they are part of the whole family effort. You may also want to seek out experienced business people you know who can help make sure you are thinking straight and not just daydreaming. Ask them to serve on your informal board of advisors so you can turn to them with questions.

3. *Have you evaluated your resources?* Take out a pad of paper and jot down all possible sources of investment capital. Include not only cash, securities, and other liquid assets, but insurance policies, the equity in your home, and retirement funds. Don't forget what the bankers refer to as NAR and NAF ("nail a relative" and "nail a friend"): your well-heeled friends and relatives could make all the difference, especially if you need a cosignature or additional equity pledged as security when applying for financing. If your dear Aunt Edna once said she would back you in a business venture, now is the time to go see her.

Consider that you may need to maintain a revenue stream while the new business is being established. Your spouse may want to land a job to make ends meet until your franchise is kicking out a salary, which may take a while. Talk to a banker and an accountant. Discuss what you are planning and ask about sources of capital, loans, investors, and angels.

4. *Have you evaluated your dreams?* Dreams provide the courage and drive that new entrepreneurs need to make the leap of faith into business ownership. But you must transform your dreams into an action plan. If you dream of being wealthy and living in a million-dollar home, turn your attention to the steps it will take to get there. If you start with owning a retail business, research how much money such a business is likely to put in your pocket, and then determine how many of those businesses and how much time you will need to achieve your dream of a million-dollar house. Use dollars in your calculations, and add time frames. Anticipate milestones along the path, and work back to where you are today. Make notes about what you need to accomplish to make it successfully to the next milestone, and before you know it you will have created what looks to others like a business plan, but to you is nothing more than your dream path.

5. *Are you ready for the physical challenge?* This question surprises a lot of people. Depending, of course, on the type of business you get involved in, business ownership can be physically demanding. Your sleep patterns may change, and you may be on your feet for 12 hours or more a day. Daily frustrations and the heightened stress of responding to unfamiliar challenges will draw on your deepest energy resources. You will need physical stamina and a healthy, positive mental outlook. I strongly recommend that as part of your preparation for owning a business, you

step up your exercise and get back to a healthy diet. You will need every ounce of energy your personal fitness can deliver.

SUMMARY NOTES

- Owning a franchise is not for everyone. Strong-willed entrepreneurs who want to do things their own way may be unhappy owning a franchise.
- Before buying a franchise, consider: the level of your motivation, how your family feels about the idea, your resources, how realistic your plans are, and whether you are ready for the physical challenge.

ACTION PLAN
Write out complete responses to the questions in this chapter (be honest here, no one else will see your answers), and file them in your business planning folder.

ATTENDING A FRANCHISE AND BUSINESS OPPORTUNITY TRADE SHOW

*J*ENNIFER HAD NEVER BEEN TO A FRANCHISE AND BUSINESS OPPOR-*tunity trade show before, but she was told it is a great place to get started in business and learn a bit about franchising and other packaged business programs. She had no plan or goals for the show, but she wanted to cruise through. However, she was overwhelmed by the atmosphere. "I got so wrapped up in the games and cookies offered at one booth I never saw most of the exhibitors. Maybe I'll go again when it comes through town next year."*

Attending a franchise and business opportunity trade show is the quickest, most enlightening way to search for the franchise program or business opportunity that best suits your needs. It can also be fun.

However, it helps to understand what you can expect at the show and to go with a plan. As many as 300 companies may be standing at their booths ready to talk to investors about their programs. Up to 10,000 people could pass through the convention center, each exploring the idea of buying a franchise or business opportunity as the ticket to business success. The effect can be dazzling: so many concepts to evaluate and hardly enough time to see them all!

Of course, many of the investors attending the show, like Jennifer, are there out of curiosity and will have no focused plan. They may be lost in the crowd and have no clue as to how to get the most out of the show. I recommend that you be different.

PREPARE FOR THE SHOW

The first step in setting yourself apart from the crowd is to prepare and set goals for the session. Decide what types of business interest you. Are you fascinated by automobiles and interested in a business that is part of that industry? Do you want a high-end consumer products business that brings you into direct contact with your customers? What are your financial resources? Do you have the money and credit to establish a retail location, or would a lower-level investment be better, perhaps a business you can operate from your home? Giving some thought to these questions will allow you to focus your time at the show on programs that fit your needs.

It's a good idea to leave your usual funky weekend attire at home and dress conservatively. Your goal is to show franchisor representatives that you are there for business. A casual business look is fine; a suit is optional, but be sure you look sharp. If possible leave the kids at home and take personal business cards if you have them. If you don't, consider having some printed up. They are inexpensive, project a business-like impression, and relieve you of having to dictate your name, address, and telephone number over and over. Don't forget your briefcase for the papers you collect, and take paper and pen for taking notes. You are not there just to pass a few idle hours and eat the free cookies. Show the representatives you meet that you are a serious prospect and there to consider their business program.

HOW TO DEVELOP AN EFFECTIVE METHOD OF ATTENDING

Plan to arrive early in the morning on one of the first days of the show. The typical franchise and business opportunity show lasts for three days, from Friday to Sunday. By Sunday, everyone is tired and spent, so try to be there on Friday (typically the least crowded day) or early Saturday (the most crowded day). This is when everyone involved should be fresh, with anticipation running high.

When you arrive at the convention center to register, take a few minutes with the show brochure to understand the floor layout, and review the list of companies that are exhibiting. Find a quiet corner with a cup of coffee and read what the show offers. Mark those companies whose offerings appeal to you and seem to fit your needs and financial resources. As you stop by their booths during the day, you can check them off and make sure you are covering all the promising companies on your list.

It is important to understand why the exhibitors are there. They consider the show a success if they collect the names of several serious, qualified candidates and come away with a list of leads for follow-up calls. I am told by franchisors that if they sell one or two franchises as the result of a trade show they can cover all of their exhibiting costs and make a profit. To get that list of hot leads they have to make about 1,000 contacts a day.

Many franchise and business opportunity shows schedule seminars for investors on subjects like "How to Buy a Franchise or Business

Opportunity" and "Financing Your Franchise Purchase." Mark the ones that look interesting and schedule time to attend them. This may be the most valuable part of your day at the trade show, especially if you actually purchase a business package.

Try to approach the exhibit floor methodically. The franchise investment possibilities are virtually endless and you may feel overwhelmed if you do not remember the interests you identified before attending the show. Stick to your plan and find as many of the exhibitors you marked off earlier in the day as you can.

It is easy to underestimate the time needed to meet with all the interesting exhibitors on your list. You might spend as much as five or ten minutes with each exhibitor and discover in a couple hours that you have met with only 10 or 15 companies, a mere fraction of those on your list.

THE RIGHT QUESTIONS

The secret is not to spend time with exhibitors whose programs are inappropriate for you or out of your financial reach. Prepare three "knock-out" questions that will allow you to eliminate those companies quickly and move on to more promising conversations. What are those questions? That depends on you and your circumstances. If you have limited resources (and who doesn't?), try "What are the minimum financial qualifications for your applicants?" or "What kind of business experience do you require?" and "Are you looking for franchisees in my town?" The franchisor's answers will tell you quickly whether their program is within your reach. If it seems to be, stay and find out more. If there is no fit, move on.

If you want to find out more about a particular franchisor, here are a few more good queries to generate useful conversation:

- How would you describe the culture in your franchise/business opportunity system? This wonderfully open-ended probe should draw a variety of responses. Every franchise and business opportunity system has a cultural character. Is it clubby, friendly, chilly, all business, or distant? Listen carefully to the answer. You will pick up some good information that does not appear in any glossy brochures.

- What are your plans for growth in this region over the next three years? The answer to this question will give you an idea of the effort and energy that the organization has committed to your market. If you get a vague answer or a grandiose statement suggesting that the company expects to take over the retail world in that modest time period, well, you've been forewarned.

- May I take a complete set of promotional material? Many exhibitors will have a limited supply of full brochures behind the table and less expensive flyers out front for the hundreds of casual visitors who stop by. Express serious interest in the investment, and ask if there are other materials you can study at home. Request a copy of the company's Uniform Franchise Offering Circular (see discussion of the UFOC in Chapter 13) or business opportunity disclosure statement. If it is not readily available, ask if the company can send you one, along with a set of promotional materials and an application package.

- Tell me about your training program. Find out how long it is (i.e., two weeks at the company headquarters and ten days in the field. . .), where it takes place, and the general subjects covered. Look for a well-organized plan that combines classroom time with field orientation. A solid training program is the mark of a careful franchisor who is interested in the business success of their franchise owners.

- Tell me about your franchisee support program. Good support from a franchisor can spell the difference between failure and success. Look for support from the very beginning, as soon as you

Franchise programs generally have extensive training for their new franchisees, in contrast to business opportunity sellers who generally offer little or no training. Business opportunity sellers prefer to provide instruction through printed materials or telephone supoport.

start to write a business plan. Will the company help you find financing? Will people be available when you are opening for business? Will someone be at the other end of the phone when things get crazy?

A question you might expect to be on this list but that isn't, is "How much money can I expect to make with one of your businesses?" This is a difficult question for a franchisor to answer. Most would like to boast about the potential of their franchise, but it is a subject that is closely regulated under the franchise laws. In addition, no franchisor knows how much you can expect to make in a franchised business. The variables—including your business acumen and industry—make such estimates impossible.

Slinging numbers at a trade show would be a misleading and unfair inducement by the seller to get you to purchase the franchise. Franchisors generally do know how their existing franchise owners have performed, and some companies will make this information available in the disclosure document. Our best advice: check it out for yourself. Go visit as many franchise owners as time and distances allow. Ask them how they have performed and whether, knowing what they now know, they would make the investment again. Their answers will be invaluable in your assessment of the franchise. (See a full discussion of this part of investigating a franchise in Chapter 24.)

It is also important to understand that a franchise trade show event is designed to make an initial contact only. It is a meeting place that operates merely to introduce sellers to potential investors. The conversation on the floor of the trade show is preliminary and rarely delves deeply into the investment itself. The more in-depth discussion usually takes place in a follow-up meeting or sometimes in a nearby hospitality suite the seller has reserved. Leave behind one of your business cards so sellers may send you additional information. And make sure that you have contact information, either a contact listing in the program or the business card of the sales representative.

TRADE SHOW RED FLAGS

Risks abound in the search for a franchise. While at the trade show, keep alert to red flags that should tell you to avoid one company or another. Here are a few:

Shouting Performance Numbers

Dollar signs have no place at a franchise trade show. They can be the source of any number of legal problems for franchisors and should be avoided by well-disciplined companies. If performance information is discussed, check out item 19 in the company's UFOC, which you will see sometime after the show. Any big talk about what you will earn should be a warning sign that this is not an experienced or well-disciplined representative. The talk may also be totally misleading.

The Hard Sell

A solid franchise investment should sell itself. If you find yourself at the receiving end of a hard sell, back slowly away.

The Start-Up Rookie

A franchising company with no track record presents risks that you should carefully evaluate. You may determine that the program is new enough and exciting enough that the potential for success outweighs the risks, but protect yourself as best you can. A new franchisor cannot offer the most attractive features of the franchise concept: a business that has been proven in the marketplace and experience that can help you handle the challenges of the business.

The Franchise Fad

Fads come and go in the franchise community. Remember that your investment needs to survive for the long term. Look out for concepts that are the flavor of the month but may have little staying power.

Limited Regional Hits

Do not assume that because a shop can sell truckloads of fresh-baked whole wheat bread in Cincinnati, the same product will move as well in Palm Beach. It may not be true, and you can't afford to prove it with your life's savings.

The Poorly-Financed Franchisor

Most franchise financial advisors will tell you that one of the most common business mistakes made in this field is for the franchisor not to have enough capital to finance its rapid growth. The resulting under-financed company is weak and may not be in a position to deliver on its promises to new franchisees. The best measure of the franchisor's financial standing is its audited financial statements, which you will find as part of the UFOC.

THE FOLLOW-UP

Expect a follow-up call or visit after the show from any company where you showed serious interest. Remember, the companies that prepared and staffed a booth invested heavily in finding you—a qualified and interested investor. The follow-up is your opportunity to dig into the investment and explore every question that might occur to you. Be diligent and skeptical in your evaluation of the information you collect from the franchisor.

IN*sight*

Your follow-up call may not come from the person you met at the show, but from
a staff representative at the company's headquarters or a regional office.
Find out who you are talking to, and get a good idea of where they fit
into the company's organization.

A franchise trade show may be your first step toward an exciting new business future. Increase the odds of your personal success by preparing carefully for the show and evaluating the opportunities presented with a detailed—and realistic—eye.

SUMMARY NOTES

- A franchise trade show can be overwhelming if you are not prepared for it.
- Prepare for the show with a battle plan.
- Ask the right questions on the floor. If there is no fit with your plan, quickly move on down the aisle.
- Look for the red flags.

- Follow up with your show contacts to confirm you are serious about finding the right franchise program.

ACTION PLAN

Find out when a good franchise and business opportunity trade show is coming to a city near you. Read a current issue of Entrepreneur *magazine or* Inc. *magazine and other business trade publications. Franchise and business opportunity trade show schedules from around the country are usually calendared there. Also try searching the Internet for trade show cities and dates. (See the next chapter for ideas on using the Internet.)*

11

RESEARCH ON
THE INTERNET

*M*ARCIE WAS DETERMINED TO FIND A BUSINESS PACKAGE THAT
*would allow her to work part-time at home
around her young children and bring in more
money for the family. Getting out of the house was difficult with the kids. She heard that a business opportunity
and franchise show was coming to the downtown arena
in a few weeks, and she wanted to find out a lot more
about the whole concept of a home business. Marcie was
a new Internet user but thought it would be a good place
to start.*

Enter the word "franchise" or "business opportunity"
into any of the competent search engines on the Internet
and you may feel a bit like Alice falling down the rabbit hole.

A Google search kicks up 1,590,000 franchise listings; on Yahoo nearly two million. "Business opportunity" brings up more than three million listings. Head down any of these pathways and you will quickly find yourself browsing through dozens of sites extolling the virtues of various franchise and business opportunities, touting association membership benefits, and describing individual franchise and business opportunity investment benefits.

WHAT TO LOOK FOR

The Internet is an essential tool in the search for the right franchise or business opportunity. It has its strengths and weaknesses, of course, but you cannot afford to overlook it. Its greatest strength is that it gives you the ability to browse for ideas and prospects. If you have leads you want to check out or if you are curious about a particular franchise, a quick search will provide at least brochure-level information about the program.

The law has been slow to catch up to the franchise regulation implications of electronic commerce on the Internet. The FTC has promised to address the rules surrounding electronic distribution of the UFOC and business opportunity disclosure documents and the posting of disclosure information on a Web site, but the rules are not yet final. Under current law, a franchisor may not comply with disclosure requirements by delivering a document in electronic form. Some states have issued regulations telling franchisors what disclaimers they must put on their sites, and you will find them in the small print of well-managed sites. In essence, the disclaimer says that the information on the site does not constitute an offer in franchise registration states. Seeing this disclaimer conveys to the experienced eye a subtle but important message: the company is receiving, and paying attention to, informed legal advice. You should wonder about franchise company sites that do not have this legal disclaimer.

HANDLING THE HIGH HYPE-TO-FACT RATIO

The Internet's weakness is the low quality and reliability of the information at its busy commercial locations. Lists of available "franchises" are littered with nonfranchised business opportunity offerings, and much of the information you see is essentially sponsored advertising. If you understand this inescapable feature of the Internet and make allowances for it, you will not be misled.

IN*sight*

The hype level tells you something about franchising and business opportunities sales. This is a market that enjoys a robust level of aggressive selling.

THE IMPORTANCE OF FOCUS

The FTC has assembled a surprisingly useful site for franchise and business opportunity investors (www.ftc.gov). Here you will find general information about franchising, the federal laws that apply to a franchise sale, and current and recent investigations and legal actions taken by the FTC against offending franchisors and business opportunity sellers.

Other popular franchise sites include:

- www.franchise.com
- www.franchise.org (the International Franchise Association)
- www.Yahoo.com /www.FranchiseSolutions.com
- www.franchiseopportunities.com
- www.entrepreneur.com (the site presented by *Entrepreneur* magazine)

These are just a start. The problem with the Internet, of course, is the sensation of trying to take a sip from a fire hose of information. The sites dedicated to franchising and business opportunities go on and on and may cause even an experienced Internet researcher to suffer from MEGO (my eyes glaze over) in no time.

The secret to effective use of the Internet for your franchise search is the same as other kinds of franchise research: focus, focus, focus. Know your targets and general interest areas. Don't be distracted by the glitter, the pop-up ads, the eager virtual experts. Plan to use your computer connection for first level contact and brochure-level information. Then roll up your sleeves and plan for person-to-person meetings and in-depth discussions about the franchise opportunity.

SUMMARY NOTES

- Use the Internet judiciously. There is a high hype-to-fact ratio at most information sites.
- The Internet is great for brochure-level information.
- Focus your search to your areas of interest.

ACTION PLAN

Spend some time on the Net and bookmark the sites that seem most helpful.

ORGANIZING THE INFORMATION YOU GATHER

*A*L WAS NOT WELL ORGANIZED IN HIS JOB LIFE, BUT THEN HE
never had a job that required him to be. He was
determined to find a good franchise. He had the
money to buy one, and he had been in contact with a
couple dozen companies. The amount of paper generated
in his search surprised him, and it had formed a few
messy piles on the floor of his bedroom. Now he was going
to a trade show and dreaded the prospect of taking more
paper home to his piles. Maybe this wasn't for him.

The franchise or business opportunity search process
can generate a lot of paper, and you will quickly become
discouraged if you do not prepare to receive and keep it in
an organized fashion. This is particularly true if you attend

franchise trade shows, which are notorious for generating piles of promotional pieces of paper. (And you wondered why they handed you that big plastic bag with handles when you walked in...!) You may also receive a stack of promotional materials when you write to franchisors for information.

IN*sight*

From the company's point of view, distributing glossy brochures is a cost of being a franchisor or business opportunity seller, and it can be quite expensive. More and more franchisors and business opportunity sellers are putting their brochure money into Web site presentations. You may find that the quality of the brochures you receive will be modest, but the Web sites will be eye-popping.

SETTING UP A FILING SYSTEM

So get prepared before you go. Set up a few files, one for each seller with internal tabs or manila folders for different subjects. Take a quick trip to an office supply store and buy a few packets of file folders, pocket files, and tab labels.

Divide each seller's file into subsections such as:

- *Promotional pieces.* Drop into this folder all of the glossy brochures, flyers, handouts, and form letters you pick up.
- *Letters, notes, contact information.* Take notes on each of the companies you visit at the trade show or elsewhere, and keep all of the personalized letters they send you, as well as copies of any letters you write. Staple into the file—or slide into a plastic sleeve—all of the sales representatives' business cards you are handed.

- *UFOC.* After you read and mark up the UFOC with any questions or comments, drop it in the file for future use. If the franchisor is a serious prospect, you will want to take this document to your attorney and accountant. It is amazing how many people buy a franchise yet never read the UFOC. You must take the time to look through this important document. If you get serious about a program, take the documents to your attorney and your CPA for review. See our discussion of the UFOC in Chapter 13.
- *Contracts.* Form contracts will be included in the UFOC, but other versions will be provided to you as you approach closing.
- *Site information, lease forms.* As you meet with landlords to review available sites for the business you have in mind, keep the information in its own section of your file.

With these files prepared ahead of time, you will be able to quickly file all the paperwork you bring home and have it easily accessible for follow-up reading.

Retain all your files until you have actually made a choice and invested in a franchise. Only then should you sort through them, keeping in your permanent records all of the documents relating to the business you purchase or remain interested in, and discarding the rest.

SUMMARY NOTES

- Prepare to organize informational materials before the franchise search begins.
- Set up labeled file folders so that you can file your papers when you get home from a trade show or other franchise or business opportunity meeting.

ACTION PLAN

Head to the supply store for the materials you will need to organize your franchise search files.

UNDERSTANDING THE UFOC

*R*OBIN INQUIRED ABOUT A FRANCHISE PROGRAM AND RECEIVED *a heavy spiral-bound book in the mail. It was at least an inch and a half thick! She did not know what it was or why they sent it. She flipped through it but did not expect to spend the time it would take to read it all.*

WHAT IS A UFOC?

Robin didn't know it yet, but what she had was the franchisee's bible: the Uniform Franchise Offering Circular or UFOC.

Like Robin, all prospective franchisees receive detailed and extensive information about the franchisor, the franchise being offered, and the franchise system. This gives you a distinct advantage over other investors. It contains sample forms of every contract you will be asked to sign, as well as a set of audited financial statements for the franchisor. In franchise circles, the UFOC is also referred to as a "franchise disclosure document" or an "offering prospectus."

The UFOC format and presentation is prescribed by state and federal law and is designed to deliver key information about the franchise investment. In it you will find 23 different items of information that are all important to your investment decision. If there is one piece of advice you take, it should be to read the UFOC carefully. Sure, it may read like an insurance policy in places, but it is a treasure trove of details for the alert investor. The good news is, all UFOC documents must be written in "plain English"—no Latin phrases, no "hereinafters," no "whereinbefores," and no run-on sentences that only a lawyer could love. At least, that's the theory.

Does everyone get a UFOC? As a practical matter, franchisors do not deliver a UFOC to everyone who applies for a franchise. The typical UFOC runs from 75 to 350 pages in length and can be expensive to reproduce in large numbers. Expect to receive a copy as you progress through the evaluation process or if you visit the company's

IN*sight*

Put yourself in the franchisor's shoes. You want to deliver a UFOC only to candidates who have been qualified and appear serious about the investment because each copy costs several dollars to reproduce. Let them know you are serious about their program and are genuinely interested in the information contained in their UFOC and you increase your chances of receiving one early in the process.

headquarters for a "first personal meeting," which will trigger the legal requirement that you receive a UFOC.

The best approach is to request a UFOC early in your discussions. If you are at all serious about a particular franchise, it makes no sense to spend time on it until you have a chance to read the UFOC.

THE SECTIONS OF THE UFOC

How do you read and comprehend a UFOC? Some sections are more important than others, but all are worth your attention.

Here is a short rundown of what to look for, section by section.

The Cover Page

This page shows the franchise logo. It also has a summary of the initial franchise fees and the total investment, followed by "Risk Factors" in all capitals. Most of the risk factors are boilerplate and address whether the franchise agreement requires the franchisee to litigate or arbitrate outside of the franchisee's home state. They also caution if the franchisor has little or no experience in business or in franchising. Make a note to discuss any such risk factor with your attorney.

Item 1: The Franchisor, Its Predecessors and Affiliates

This is a concise overview of the franchisor, its formal corporate name and state of incorporation, and its background, business experience, predecessors, and affiliates. It tells you how long the company has been offering franchises and gives a general description of the franchisee's potential competition. Read the franchisor's business record carefully.

Item 2: Business Experience

This section gives you a bare-bones five-year outline of the business experience of the franchisor's key executives. It's just the facts: title, employer, dates of employment, and city. Note if there are any gaps in the employment history (such as might be created by some time out of work).

Item 3: Litigation

This section requires the franchisor to reveal details about specific types of litigation that may be "material" (important) to prospective franchisees. If in the past ten years the company itself or any of its directors or officers listed in item 2 have been defendants in cases involving claims of franchise law, securities law, fraud, unfair or deceptive trade practices, or comparable allegations, you will see it described here. You will also see arbitration actions listed in this section.

Don't be alarmed if there are one or two cases disclosed here. It is a rare franchisor, or one that has not been in the franchising business long, that has no litigation to disclose in item 3. In this great country anyone can file a lawsuit alleging anything, so the cases disclosed may not convey the right impression of the company or its dispute resolution style. On the other hand, an item 3 that discloses many cases may tell you a lot about the company. The best approach is to make a note to discuss with your own attorney and your franchisor representative any questions you have about disclosures in this item. You may also want to ask any existing franchisees you interview about the company's litigation history. They can probably shed light on what the company's litigation style means to franchisees.

Item 4: Bankruptcy

If there is a bankruptcy in the ten-year background of the franchisor, its predecessors, affiliates, partners, or officers, you will see it briefly described in item 4.

Item 5: Initial Franchise Fee

This section details all moneys paid to the franchisor prior to the time the franchisee opens for business. Typically, the franchisor imposes an initial franchise fee that is a lump sum payment—as much as $20,000, $30,000, or more—to be made at the time the franchise agreement is signed. Look for other fees, such as training fees, that may be included, and the circumstances in which they might be refundable.

Item 6: Other Fees

The chart in item 6 summarizes all of the recurring or isolated fees that the franchisee must pay to the franchisor or its affiliates during the course of the franchise relationship. The royalty is listed, of course. The chart also includes any continuing advertising contributions to an advertising fund or otherwise, cooperative advertising organizations that charge advertising fees, transfer fees, and audit costs.

Item 7: Initial Investment

This section of the UFOC is one of the most important for your planning purposes. In chart form, it summarizes the total initial expenses you can expect when opening the franchised business. It tells you what categories of expenses are typical, to whom payments are to be made, and when they are due. It also tells you whether payments are refundable under any circumstances. Use these figures when preparing your own business plan, but check with a good accountant and existing franchisees in the system to see if there are other expenses you should anticipate that are not included in item 7. For instance, if you borrow a substantial portion of the investment, you will have debt service to anticipate that will not appear in this disclosure document. Consider this item as the starting point in your financial planning.

Item 8: Restrictions on Sources of Products and Services

The area of product sourcing is one of the most important aspects of franchise operations, but it is often well hidden. Imagine that you are considering a franchise for an ice cream shop that sells a premium ice cream that is manufactured especially for the franchise system.

There is only one source of the product, the franchisor. You are required by the franchise agreement to purchase only from the designated source. Would you know whether $11.35 per tub is a reasonable price for ice cream inventory? What will you do if the franchisor raises their prices and cuts down your (already razor-thin) margins? Some franchisees feel trapped by a confining supply arrangement where they have no opportunity to seek out a competitive price. Supply arrangements are described in this item but may not paint the entire picture for you.

Item 9: Franchisee's Obligations

This item is nothing more than a cross-reference chart showing you where certain subjects are addressed in the franchise agreement.

Item 10: Financing

If the franchisor offers financing, either directly or indirectly, you will find it detailed here. It should lay out the terms of the financing in chart form and specify which portion of the purchase qualifies for the financing. Copies of any loan documents will be included as exhibits.

Item 11: Franchisor's Obligations

This provides a lengthy recital of the promises made by the franchisor, the services they will supply to you in the course of the franchise relationship, and details about some of the training and other programs offered. This is the longest section of the UFOC and it contains a wealth of information. Among the topics addressed are the pre-opening and post-opening services to be provided by the franchisor, the time that typically elapses between the date of signing the franchise agreement and opening the business, the specifications for any computerized cash registers or computers necessary in the business, and a detailed description of the training program.

Item 12: Territory

This is a description of any territorial rights granted as a part of the franchise agreement. It is fair to say that most, but not all, franchise systems include some form of territorial protection for the franchisee. The key point for the prospective franchisee is to read this section carefully and without the natural assumptions you may have of these intangible concepts. For instance it may include a promise by the franchisor that says something like, "We will not develop ourselves or grant franchises to others to develop another franchise in your territory." Does this mean that you have absolute exclusivity in the territory? No. In fact, it is a rather narrow promise that prevents the establishment of competing units in your area, but does not prevent the franchisor from selling product to customers in your territory. Ask your attorney to review the promises in this section so that you are clear on the nature of the rights you are receiving. They are important.

Item 13: Trademarks

It has been said that the trademark is the cornerstone of the franchise relationship. Item 13 provides some key details about the primary trademarks associated with the franchise package. First it tells you whether the trademark has been registered with the U.S. Patent and Trademark Office. While that registration is not necessary for a protectable trademark, it is an important step for the franchisor, and if it has not been done, it tells you and your attorney a lot. Having an unregistered mark may increase your risks that someone else with the same mark can claim superior legal rights and force you and the franchisor to find another trade name. If the franchisor has any litigation pending that pertains to the marks, it is described here, as are promises made by the franchisor to protect franchisees from claims of trademark infringement by third parties. Make sure that your attorney reviews item 13 and advises you of any apparent problems.

Item 14: Patents, Copyrights, and Proprietary Information

The majority of UFOCs contain boilerplate language in this section because so few franchise programs have patent rights that pertain to the franchise. What is usually protected by copyright are the operations manual and other printed advertising and operating materials. There is also language in this section protecting the "trade secrets" and other "proprietary rights" of the franchisor in various aspects of the franchised business.

Item 15: Obligation to Participate in the Actual Operation of the Franchise Business

If the contract requires you to be present at the business for a certain number of hours each week, or that a trained manager supervise the operation at all times, it should be disclosed here.

Item 16: Restrictions on What the Franchisee May Sell

If you will be required to sell only approved products, or only those supplied to you by approved suppliers, it will say so here.

Item 17: Renewal, Termination, Transfer, and Dispute Resolution

This multipage chart provides the reader a full cross-reference to the franchise agreement along with a summary of the key legal provisions relating to renewal (what happens at the end of the contract term), termination (the circumstances under which you and the franchisor may choose to end the contract before its expiration), transfer (the restrictions on your right to sell all or part of your franchised business), and dispute resolution (where and how legal disputes will be resolved). These topics are the most legally intense sections of the franchise agreement and deserve careful review by your attorney.

Item 18: Public Figures

This section describes the terms of any endorsement or other involvement by a well-known figure who is promoting the franchise.

Item 19: Earnings Claims

This item may provide some of your most important clues to answering the question, "How much money does one of these babies make?" Franchisors are not required to supply any performance information about their program, but if they do, it must be disclosed here. Only about 20 percent of all UFOCs contain performance information. There could be a number of reasons for a company leaving this disclosure blank. It may be that they are concerned about potential misrepresentations and legal liability if they list performance figures for their existing franchisees. It may also be that the performance statistics do not tell a compelling story, and the company does not want to focus your attention on the low performance of its franchised businesses. If you do find performance information, be sure to use it when you prepare your business plan. Then supplement the bare statistics with franchisee interviews. If the company does not disclose anything, find out why, and press for performance information from other sources. Again, existing franchisees are the best place to start.

Item 20: List of Outlets

This section includes a series of charts about the growth or contraction of the franchise system for the prior three years, as well as information about existing company-owned units and projected growth of the system during the coming year. There is an attached list of the names, addresses, and telephone numbers of current franchisees, as well as a list of the names and the last-known addresses and telephone numbers of all franchisees who have left the system during the prior year or have not been in contact with the franchisor for at least ten weeks. These lists are often attached as exhibits to the UFOC. Find out from these former franchise owners why they left and whether it was related to shortcomings in the program itself.

Item 21: Financial Statements

The law requires that a franchisor attach to the body of the UFOC as an exhibit a copy of its financial balance sheet and operating statements for the prior three years, all of which must be audited (or "certified") by a certified public accountant. If the franchisor has been in existence for less than three years, or has only recently begun franchising, you may find fewer than three years of financial statements. However, the company is required to provide at least one certified statement, even if it is only an opening balance sheet. Make sure your accountant sees this information. You want to make sure the franchisor is on solid financial footing and in business for the long haul.

Item 22: Contracts

You will find a description of all the contracts you need to sign in order to purchase the franchise in this item. Copies of the contracts will also be attached to the UFOC as an exhibit. If the franchisor provides loan documents, equipment, or real estate leases, they are also included in an exhibit, along with a sample franchise agreement form. Before you close on the transaction, make sure your attorney has a chance to review all of these contracts.

Item 23: Receipt

The UFOC requires that two receipts be attached to it, one for the franchisee and the other for the franchisor. This is important for the franchisor in case they have to prove they delivered a disclosure document to you and that you received it. (Was it at least ten business days before you signed the franchise agreement?) You must sign and date the receipt.

That's a lot of investment information in one document—and well worth reading through it.

SUMMARY NOTES

- The UFOC is a key document in your search for a franchise.
- READ the UFOC!
- Have professionals help you with parts of this document.
- Review the various sections of the UFOC. Some are more important than others.
- The UFOC does not contain ALL of the information you need to evaluate the franchise.

ACTION PLAN

Get a UFOC—any UFOC—and flip through it to see how it is organized and where to find key information.

14

FIVE GREAT QUESTIONS *NOT* ANSWERED IN THE UFOC

*E**LLEN SLOGGED THROUGH THE UFOC FOR THE FRANCHISE SHE was interested in and was proud of herself. She had every reason to be impressed by the program and wondered if there was anything else she needed to dig into. Surely, she thought, this huge tome told her everything she needed to know. Right?*

THE UFOC DOES NOT DELIVER EVERYTHING

Ellen makes a mistake if she assumes that the UFOC will tell her everything she needs to know about the franchise investment. It is designed by regulators to deliver information that they consider "material" to the investment—that is, information that should be important to the investor. However, there are some gaping holes in the

UFOC, key pieces of information it does not convey that are material to your purchase decision. Take a look at five of the most important areas. There may be more, depending on the type of business you are buying.

Pricing/Product Distribution

Item 8 of the UFOC delivers some of the product and pricing information you need, but the guidelines for franchisors to follow in preparing this section are complex and cumbersome resulting in confusing disclosures that are not particularly helpful. After all, smooth product sourcing, the savings on prices available to franchisees based on large group purchases, and carefully considered product specifications are

---

IN*sight*

I talked to a franchisee of an ice cream concept who was beside himself. He has an MBA and thought his business looked great on paper. He liked the taste of the product, the well-designed brand name, the modern look of the stores, the sales figures he had seen, and the location in an enclosed mall without a food court. What he didn't count on was the price of the premium ice cream, which, under the terms of the franchise agreement, could be purchased only from the franchisor. The price was way too high, but he didn't realize it until he got into the business and learned about wholesale ice cream prices. The president of the company told him that there was no UFOC because, "We are not a public company." "How was I to know about that?" he says. Now he is saddled with an expensive business that is breaking even but not making much of a profit, and he is embarrassed to admit this could happen to an MBA.

---

all fundamental business reasons for buying a franchise. If this part of the business is not working well, there may be little reason to go into the franchise.

Make a point of exploring product dynamics with the franchisees you meet. Press the franchisor representatives about purchasing arrangements, any buying cooperatives in your area, and pricing strategies. Check the franchise agreement and any other paperwork from the franchisor describing product matters. In many franchises this is the economic engine of the business. It never hurts to look under the hood and make sure it is running well.

Franchisee Associations

Nowhere in the UFOC is a franchisor required to disclose the existence of a franchisee association or advisory council. Yet this is an important aspect of the franchise program for a new investor. The presence of a strong association that is well attended and governed by franchisees is an attractive asset of any franchise program.

IN*sight*

A franchisee association or council organizes and provides to the franchisor and all franchisees a valuable franchisee viewpoint of the business. Franchisee associations generally meet on a regular basis, and the prudent franchisor listens carefully to the advice and recommendations offered. They can provide new investors a knowledgeable perspective independent of the franchisor and an in-depth evaluation of the whole franchise organization.

I have long suspected that omitting any mention of a franchisee association in the UFOC is due to the swift internal political waters surrounding franchisee associations. Some associations are created by the franchisor and promoted by the company; others are "renegade associations" created by the franchisees and resented by the franchisor. Ask current franchisees about the role they play through an association or a franchisee council.

Training

One of the keys to franchisee success is solid training. The UFOC will give you some of the basic facts, including a chart outlining the sections of the training, who teaches the sections, the experience of the trainers, how much time is devoted to each topic, and where the training takes place. However, you need assurances about the program that cannot be delivered in a disclosure document. Is the training effective? Do franchisees feel that they are well prepared to run a successful business upon completing it? Is the training based on current thinking, and is it the best available in the field? Is it complete, and how much of it is hands-on, under supervision? Be sure you explore these ideas with franchisees and your franchisor representatives.

Market for Product/Service

This is a basic but intangible question that is difficult to address in a disclosure document: Is the market for the product or service a strong one? Is the growth of the market for the business on the rise or decline?

Franchisor Support

The language in a franchise agreement that describes the level of the franchisor's continuing support may be surprising. You are likely to find something like: "The franchisor will provide such continuing advice and support as it deems appropriate in its absolute discretion."

How's *that* for reassurance?! Attorneys for franchisors learned decades ago that specific promises of support in the franchise agreement, such as quarterly meetings, monthly newsletters, and regular telephone calls, would lead to legal trouble when the franchisor's business practices changed. And they always change. The result is the smallest, most flexible promise of support imaginable.

Even though the promises might be modest, the practice is important. Find out exactly—from franchisees and the franchisor's representatives—what the company does for its new franchisees when they are planning to locate the business, when they are hiring staff, and during the opening and start-up phase. Is help available? Is it responsive? Will the franchisor be there to help if and when things go wrong?

SUMMARY NOTES

- As lengthy as it is, the UFOC will not deliver all the information you need to know about a franchise program.
- Look to some key topics for more information: product distribution, franchisee associations, training, the market for the product and/or service, and franchisee support by the franchisor.

ACTION PLAN

Write a single-page list of questions and topics you want to discuss with any franchisor representative you meet. Ask your attorney and accountant if you should add other questions to your list.

THE KEY SECTIONS OF THE FRANCHISE AGREEMENT

*B*ILL RECEIVED HIS FRANCHISE AGREEMENT AND FIGURED HE'D *just look it over himself. Why hire an attorney? He knew attorneys could be expensive. After all, the contract was in English and looked straightforward to him. Sure it was long and the language was a little dense, but it was registered under Bill's state franchise law and seemed to be fully described in the UFOC. What could go wrong?*

UNDERSTANDING THE BASIC DYNAMIC OF THE FRANCHISE AGREEMENT

Bill is setting himself up for an expensive lesson. The agreement that grants a franchisee the right to operate a business in the franchisor's system is a complex commercial contract. It is designed to create a continuing business relationship that could span 20 years or more. It grants a panoply of intangible "intellectual property" rights, describes product and service standards, and sets the ground rules for the transfer, renewal, and termination of the relationship.

This agreement is not an easy document to read or understand, and it makes sense to take it to an attorney who can help you understand it in detail. While the size, shape, and style of franchise agreements are tailored to each system, many of their basic features are universal. You will be well ahead of the franchise game if you comprehend the basic legal dynamics of this complex contract.

KEY PROVISIONS CONSIDERED

Intellectual Property Rights

A franchise agreement has been described as a trademark license with overdrive. It grants to the franchisee the limited right to use the trademarks, techniques, procedures, trade dress, and know-how that comprise the franchise system. These rights are "limited" so that the franchisor can preserve their ownership rights of trademarks, copyrights, and trade secrets.

IN*sight*

A franchise is at its essence the licensing of intellectual property. All of the valuable information delivered to the franchisee, from the trademark, to the operating manuals, to the techniques taught in training, to the color designs of a retail franchise, is a form of intangible intellectual property.

Look closely at these terms:

Trademark. This a word, name, phrase, symbol, logo, or in some cases a design that traditionally represents the source of a product or service. A leading example is McDonald's® brand sandwiches, including the famous Big Mac® sandwich. A trademark owner has the legal right to license other people to use the trademark, and those licenses generally require correct display of the mark. If the colors of red and yellow in the McDonald's golden arches brand name are a bit off—if they turn out maroon and gold—you can expect the trademark owner to object. A "service mark" is the same thing as a trademark, but it specifically identifies a service, not a product.

Franchise System Techniques and Procedures. In a franchise system these terms denote the specifications, equipment, and routines that are part of the franchise rights and obligations. They are usually found in an operating manual provided by the franchisor. In a restaurant franchise for instance, the operating manual details the preparation of all menu items and their components, as well as things such as the timing of cooking and the temperature of cooking oil. Equipment specifications are included, as well as the uniform attire of employees. Many of these techniques that are not obvious to the public may be claimed by the franchisor as *trade secrets*, which are confidential and not to be disclosed. All franchisees need to be aware of claimed trade secrets and take steps to keep them confidential.

Trade Dress. This is a legal term that describes the appearance of a product, product packaging, or the distinctive style of a building or restaurant. Trade dress may be protected under the law in the same fashion as a trademark. What does this mean to a franchisee? If you operate a restaurant franchise in a building with a distinctive color design or roof line, those features may have to be changed if you leave the system because they are *owned* by the franchisor.

Know-How. This is often used to describe the knowledge and entire set of techniques that go into a franchise system. It includes the franchisor's experience in business and their knowledge of the bumps and bruises of the marketplace and how to avoid them, and it is imparted to the franchisee in a healthy franchise system.

Copyright. This is the legal protection of an original work that is fixed in a tangible form, including books, songs, plays, software and all printed material. The legal copyright protects the author's exclusive right to use and exploit the value of the work. It cannot be published, copied, or used without the author's permission. An author—and this is important—cannot protect an idea but can claim a copyright for the original expression of an idea (like a novel or a franchise operations manual). The franchise system's operations manual, advertising, and other printed material may be copyright protected by the franchisor. As a franchisee you may be restricted in the ways you can use and exploit these materials for your own purposes.

Patent. A patent is a property right, secured in the U.S. Constitution, protecting the rights to an invention, new device, or innovation. As with a trademark, the owner has the right to license the use of their patented device to other people.

License Rights

The franchisee receives the right to use and display the trademark, or a family of trademarks, only as the franchisor authorizes, and only during the term of the franchise agreement. This means that all signs displaying the mark, and all printed materials, vehicles, and even Web locations used by the franchisee must be approved in form, color, and design by the franchisor.

Although this is a point of some contention in the franchise community, the "goodwill" of the franchised business represented by the trademark—which is to say much of the goodwill of the business itself—remains in the ownership of the franchisor, not the franchisee. In that sense, a franchise agreement is similar to a commercial lease: at the end of the lease term the property that is granted reverts completely to the owner, not the tenant.

The same may be said of any of the other intellectual property of the franchise system. Its use is licensed only in the manner prescribed and only for the term of the franchise agreement. When the franchise agreement is expired or terminated, all rights to use the trademarks, copyrighted material, patents, and/or trade secrets will also cease.

Contract Flexibility Over Time

How does the franchise relationship handle the marketplace changes that occur in the franchise system over a number of years? The changed appearance of American business establishments in the past 20 years, or even 10 years, is dramatic. Look at a picture of a McDonald's restaurant or Holiday Inn from the 1980s. They've definitely changed!

Franchise relationships must allow for change over time, and they do it by incorporating a reference in the contract to a living, changing set of policies, standards, guidance, and know-how contained in a confidential set of documents, usually called operating manuals. The manuals are typically updated as changes in the system occur or new policies are adopted.

The franchise agreement also usually describes a dynamic franchise system that changes over time. The parties stipulate that many aspects of the franchise will require alteration as the years go by.

Franchise agreements accommodate changes over time by expressly anticipating them, while assuring the franchisee that the *fundamental* rights of the contract will not change. While franchisees clearly want to receive their full contract rights and the undiluted benefit of their bargain, they also want the franchisor to take the lead in keeping their business concept fresh and competitive in the marketplace. Obviously, this creates something of a dynamic legal tension for the franchisee and franchisor. What is fundamental and what is allowed to change over time?

While there is no easy answer, the courts and franchise systems ask whether a particular change is "material" to the franchisee's business. Is a proposed change so important (or fundamental) that it would have affected the franchisee's decision to purchase the franchise if they had known that such a change would be made to the program? If it is material or fundamental to the franchise, it may be in violation of the contract's promises to the franchisee.

Product Standards

The essential genius of franchising is the delivery of consistent products or services through independent businesses licensed to operate under a universal display mark. Isn't it remarkable that a *Big Mac*® sandwich purchased at a McDonald's in Bangor, Maine, tastes the same as one bought in Hawaii or Australia? What is more remarkable is that all of the ingredients and sandwich components are provided by unaffiliated, third-party suppliers to the McDonald's system.

The franchise agreement addresses the requirements of product and service supply in one of several different ways, reflecting varying degrees of control that the company needs to exercise over the delivery of the products or services of the franchised business. In some systems, of course, the franchisor is the manufacturer of the product line carried by the franchisee, and the franchise is itself a "product franchise" through which independent franchisees distribute the line.

In most business format franchise programs, franchisees are required to purchase only from suppliers who have received the company's prior written approval. If the franchisee wants to buy product from a supplier who has not received approval, the franchise agreement requires that an application must be made to the franchisor. This way the franchisor can assure that all suppliers to the system are capable of delivering specialized product and that system standards are not eroded through poor supply selections (which are often driven by price considerations) made by franchisees.

An even-handed supplier approval process also allows the franchisor to control quality without unreasonably restricting supplier access to its system of franchise buyers, which could have serious antitrust implications for the franchisor. An unreasonably restrictive supply arrangement might injure competition among suppliers to franchisees. Injury to competition is what antitrust laws were designed to combat.

Transfer

Can the franchisee build up the business and then sell it to another person? In most systems the franchisee can sell the business only if the franchisor issues written permission, and permission is generally granted by a franchisor only after reviewing the qualifications of the prospective buyer. Most franchisors apply the same standards of qualification on the proposed transferee (the buyer) as they apply to new applicants.

If the transferee does not measure up, the franchisor has every right to deny consent to the transfer. The courts have made it clear that a franchisor has a legitimate interest in preventing its franchised businesses from being owned by business people who are undercapitalized, lack necessary levels of business experience, or fail to meet the company's objective qualifications.

The transfer, or assignment, sections of the typical franchise agreement are the most lengthy and dense legalese of the entire contract, but are also the most important to the value of the franchisee's business. Your ability to sell your business and pull out your sweat equity is essential to the original decision to purchase the franchise.

It surprises many franchisees to learn that the transfer language of the contract may cover events that do not amount to the sale of the business, such as taking in a new partner, granting stock in an existing corporation that is the franchisee, the death of a minority owner of a franchise, and shifting ownership of the unit's assets to a newly formed corporation or limited liability company. All of these events require the prior written consent of the franchisor, if the contract's transfer provisions are typical.

CORPORATE OWNERSHIP

Private Corporations, Limited Liability Companies (LLCs), and Personal Guarantees

Most franchisors allow an individual investor to create these legal entities to serve as the formal franchisee under the franchise agreement. It often makes sense: create an LLC to hold the franchise rights, sign the franchise agreement, hold the assets of the operation, and accommodate multiple ownership and various positions and roles. However, there is usually one catch, and it's a significant one: under the franchise agreement you will be asked to personally guarantee to the franchisor the obligations of your new legal entity.

"Wait a minute," you say, "my lawyer told me that the main reason for creating an LLC was to shield my personal assets from the liabilities of the business!" That's right. The personal guarantee, if required by the franchisor, defeats that objective, at least insofar as you wanted to be shielded from the claims of the franchisor. If it is narrowly drafted, the guarantee should not defeat your objective relating to other aspects of the business.

What does this personal guarantee mean as a practical matter? Suppose your business falls on difficult times and you are unable to pay the royalties, and perhaps the franchisor terminates your franchise or you close the business. The franchisor will have legal claim for royalties and other damages against the LLC *and* you personally, as well as others who have guaranteed the obligations of your legal entity.

Right of First Refusal

Many franchise agreements reserve to the franchisor a "right of first refusal." This means that if you receive a formal offer to purchase your business, you must present the offer to the franchisor and allow them the opportunity to purchase your business on the same terms. This

---

IN*sight*

Most franchisors include a right of first refusal in their franchise agreements in order to control ownership of the franchised businesses and to buy out a franchisee if it fits with the company's business plans for that area. However, it is a right rarely exercised by a franchisor.

---

allows the franchisor to maintain control over the buying and selling of its franchises, but also draws criticism from franchisees who believe that it hampers their ability to attract a serious buyer. What buyer wants to go through the effort of putting together a detailed purchase offer, only to have the franchisor take it out from under them?

Termination

Oh, the dreaded termination section! It seems to rattle on *ad nauseam*, listing dozens of situations in which the franchisor may terminate the relationship, while rarely including even *one* circumstance in which the franchisee may terminate the relationship. Franchisors generally have only one enforcement tool, the threat of termination. They describe it at length, but use it gingerly.

Here are some of the typical termination grounds you will see in a franchise agreement, with notes on what to look out for:

Business Abandonment. Make sure you understand how abandonment is defined. You don't want a spring vacation to amount to abandonment of your business.

Criminal Conviction. How is a crime defined here? Is it a felony or any crime? The franchisor wants to protect their reputation if the franchisee commits a crime.

Many franchise agreements also include the broader termination grounds of the franchisee committing an act that injures the goodwill of the trademark. Plan to discuss this provision with your attorney.

Lying on the Application. If you mislead the company during the application process, it wants to reserve the right to terminate the relationship.

Bankruptcy. If your business does declare bankruptcy, the franchisor wants to be able to terminate the contractual relationship. This termination provision is often set to occur "automatically" if bankruptcy is declared, but in fact a whole body of federal bankruptcy law will take effect immediately. Bankruptcy legal specialists caution that the law may not allow the franchisor to terminate after a bankruptcy, regardless of what the contract says.

Termination after Notice. Most franchise agreements allow the franchisor to terminate the relationship if the franchisee receives notice of any default and does not correct the problem within a reasonable amount of time. The typical time to cure is 30 days, but it certainly could be a longer or shorter period, depending on the nature of the default.

> Termination after notice is how most franchise terminations occur. If you receive a default notice that warns of the possible termination of your franchise rights, do not file it away. Respond to it immediately.

The franchise agreement, drafted by lawyers in the interests of franchisors, allows them to protect their trademarks, systems, and other intellectual property if a franchisee abuses, misuses, or misappropriates any portion of the franchised business. At the same time, exacting termination language allows the franchisor to protect other franchisees.

Look at it this way: if a franchisee on the other side of your small town is running a slovenly or dirty operation, your *own* business will suffer. That is the other sharp blade of the two-edged sword of franchising: you operate under the same trademark as many other operators; their businesses are indistinguishable from yours in the eye of the customer.

Most franchisees dislike the seemingly overbearing language of their own franchise agreement but are the first to insist that the franchisor use those rights to enforce system standards against another owner who is not doing the job.

The franchise laws of about 19 jurisdictions impose standards of termination that preempt conflicting language of a franchise agreement, allowing for termination or failure to renew only when the franchisor has good cause, as that term is defined in the statute. These statutes come into play if you get into a tangle with the franchisor and they notify you that your franchise is or will be canceled.

DISPUTE RESOLUTION PROVISIONS

The truth is: franchising tends to generate disputes. The interests of franchisor and franchisee are fundamentally at odds in a number of ways. Remember, the franchisor receives royalties based on a percentage of the *gross sales* of the business, *before* expenses are paid; the franchisee takes money home at the end of the day if they maximize profits, *after* expenses are paid. Franchisors therefore push for higher sales; franchisees for better profits. We discuss resolving franchisor/franchisee disputes in Chapter 19.

One measure of excellence in franchising is the ability of the franchisor to avoid the courtroom when they must enforce the terms of its

IN*sight*

Franchisors have additional motivation to avoid a courtroom or an arbitration procedure: disclosure. The UFOC requires that a franchisor disclose in item 3 certain lawsuits and arbitration procedures during the prior ten years as well as the terms of any settlement of those actions.

franchise agreements. The contract may contain a provision that requires the parties to submit all disputes to an arbitration process before any lawsuit may be filed. Where must that arbitration take place? Many franchise agreements specify that the process take place at the American Arbitration Association office closest to the franchisor headquarters. That means you have to travel to the franchisor's backyard in order to resolve a dispute.

Even if there is no arbitration language in place, the franchise agreement may specify where a lawsuit must be filed if either party makes a legal claim under the contract. Franchisee attorneys generally resist accepting language mandating that legal actions must be filed in the home jurisdiction of the franchisor.

Remember, no prospective franchisee should attempt to fully comprehend a franchise agreement without the benefit of legal counsel. Your attorney is far more familiar with the complexities and limitations of contract law and can advise you about the obligations and rights it stipulates.

For all of the attention the contract receives at the start of the relationship, it should not loom large in your daily business. When everything is going well, the franchised business is succeeding, and your relationship with the franchisor is on solid footing, that carefully evaluated franchise agreement—the foundation of your business investment—will not even come out of the drawer. All solid foundations are supposed to work that way.

SUMMARY NOTES

- Take the proposed franchise agreement to an attorney. It's important.
- It is also important to understand some of the basic dynamics of a franchise agreement, such as intellectual property, license rights, product standards, transfer, and termination.

- If the business works out well, the contract will not come out of the drawer. If problems arise, it is the key to resolving any disputes.

ACTION PLAN

Look immediately for a good attorney. Ask current franchisees or friends in business who they use, or contact your state bar association.

FRANCHISOR FINANCIAL INFORMATION IN THE UFOC
(AND HOW DO I READ THIS GOBBLEDEGOOK?)

*E*RIC NEVER HAD A HEAD FOR NUMBERS, BUT THOUGHT HE WAS *pretty good at judging the financial status of a company by its balance sheets. Now the UFOC gave him an opportunity to do just that for the home health care franchise he was evaluating. But he had never seen a franchisor balance sheet and operating statement before and was not sure what to make of them. So he decided to take them to his accountant. Something told him this was too important to be left to his amateur accounting skills.*

FRANCHISOR FINANCIAL DISCLOSURES

Eric's instincts are serving him well. Item 21 of the UFOC requires franchisors to supply two years of audited balance sheets and three years of audited operational statements. This is extremely important information for a prospective franchisee and should not be left to an amateur evaluation. It shows whether the franchisor is well capitalized, how well they are managing their cash flow, and whether the company is healthy and profitable. In short it is a snapshot of the franchisor's finances, and it is invaluable to you.

You are considering entering into a 5, 10, or even 20-year relationship when you execute a franchise agreement. You want to know whether the franchisor has staying power and will be there for the duration.

AUDITS ACCORDING TO GAAP

What does it mean that a financial statement is "audited"? It means that a certified public accountancy firm has independently reviewed the company's books and expressed its professional opinion in writing that the financial statements accurately reflect the company's financial position and have been prepared in accordance with Generally Accepted Accounting Principles (GAAP)—the standard financial statement rules.

This audit opinion is a big deal in the world of accountants. It is the highest level of review that a CPA conducts (the other two are a Compilation Report and a Review Report), and it is as close as you're going to get to an independent third party approving the accuracy of a set of financials. You can usually rely on the accuracy of an audited statement.

IN*sight*

The auditors must consent to the inclusion of their report in the UFOC. They go through a rigorous process of inspecting the company's records for the period they are auditing, as required by the standards of the accounting profession. A Compilation Report or Review Report does not involve that level of accounting scrutiny.

So you peek at the exhibits in the back of your UFOC and there they are, the franchisor's financials. They are a sea of numbers. Now what do you do? Well, it goes without saying that most people have not made a study of how to read a financial statement. Now is not the time to start. Take the UFOC to an accountant, preferably a CPA, and have them conduct a review. You are going to need the services of a good accountant anyway when it comes time to plan the business, make some projections, and create a business road map, so asking for a quick review of a set of financials is a good first step. Talk to the accountant about what it is you need and how much it will cost. Can't afford the full Cadillac review? Then ask how much half an hour of time costs. Present the financials and ask the accountant to go over them slowly and explain what they mean to an experienced eye.

ACCOUNTANT'S ANALYSIS TIPS

I asked Roger Heymann of Heymann, Suissa and Stone, P.C. of Rockville, Maryland—one of the leading small business accounting firms on the East Coast—to summarize some of the lingo you may encounter in this session and to recommend what to listen for and what to ask. Here is what Roger says:

"For a prospective franchisee, there are three major points to keep in mind when looking at financial statements. These are: look at the relevant ratio analyses, pay close attention to footnotes, and conduct an industry analysis.

"Qualitative information from financial statements can be gathered by performing a *ratio analysis*, which expresses the relationship among selected financial statement data. As a franchisee, you want to pay close attention to relevant ratios, which may include the *current ratio, quick ratio, inventory turnover,* and *return on assets ratio*. Current ratio and quick ratio measure short-term debt-paying ability. Inventory turnover presents the liquidity of inventory. Return on assets ratio measures the overall profitability of assets.

"The second major point is to pay close attention to the footnotes to the financial statement. These provide the additional key information that supplements the principal financial statement. There are two types of footnotes. First, the *major accounting policies* of the business have to be identified and explained. They tell an investor what method the company chooses to present its accounts in the financial statement. For example, the *cost of goods sold* expense method will be included in this type of footnote. The second kind of footnote provides additional information that cannot be placed in the main body of the financial statement. For example, the maturity date or interest rate of a particular loan will be stated in the footnotes.

"The last major point is to conduct an *industry analysis*. A company's financial statements can tell you how well the business ran in the past, but not how well it has been doing in the context of a specific industry. Therefore, an industry analysis is needed to put the figures in perspective."

EVALUATING THE FRANCHISOR'S FINANCIAL STANDING

Now that an accountant has advised you about the franchisor's financial standing, how do you evaluate it in your investment decisions? Take a look at a common example. Say the franchisor is a subsidiary of a well-known corporation, but is showing only a small net worth on an opening balance sheet with no operating history. What do you make of that?

First, understand why you are looking at a franchisor with a small net worth. When a well-established corporation considers franchising for the first time, the attorneys explain that it will need to provide a set of audited financial statements for the UFOC. If the company has never prepared an audited statement in the past, this can pose an extremely expensive problem. Auditors have to go over the corporation's old books in painful detail, and probably charge the corporation an arm and a leg. On top of that, the company is concerned about litigation arising out of the franchise program and figures that a subsidiary corporation will add an additional level of protection for the corporation. So the company decides it will be cheaper and smarter to create a new corporation to serve as the franchisor. A newly formed franchisor must provide only an audited opening balance sheet, which is a relatively simple matter for the auditor to complete. If the franchise program results in litigation, the assets of the established corporation are shielded.

This is perfectly legal, and quite common in franchising. When a thinly capitalized franchisor files in one of the registration states, however, it will probably be required to provide a surety bond to the state or make some other protective financial arrangement for investors as a condition of registration.

What does a surety bond do for franchisees? Imagine you have paid a $30,000 initial franchise fee, and the franchisor tells you that it cannot provide the promised training because it is low on funds and the training managers have quit. You request your money back, and the franchisor says it does not have that amount of cash in its accounts. In that situation you would probably qualify to apply to be reimbursed under the surety bond on file with state authorities. It makes it relatively easy to be reimbursed for the investment of an initial fee if the franchisor goes out of business or is otherwise unable to perform basic obligations because it has no substantial assets. Without a protection like a surety bond, you may have no recourse at all, except filing a lawsuit against the franchisor and its principals.

Whether or not you are in a registration state, a low franchisor net worth increases the risks you are taking when you invest in a franchised business. If you are looking at a young program that has not been in operation very long, it may have an extremely low net worth. The profit potential of buying a franchise from a new concept may be high, but the concomitant risks should be part of your calculation when you evaluate any franchise investment.

The regulation of franchise sales is not designed to make all franchise investments safe. In order not to interfere unnecessarily in the marketplace, franchise regulation is designed to deliver all pertinent information into the hands of the investor, and then step back so that the investor can make an informed decision. That leaves a substantial burden on the prospective franchisee to consider all of the relevant information.

SUMMARY NOTES

- The UFOC requires the inclusion of the franchisor's audited financial statements.
- Audits are generally presented by independent accountants, and they confirm that the numbers are prepared and presented according to the standards adopted in the business accounting industry known as Generally Accepted Accounting Principles (GAAP).
- Accountants conduct a ratio analysis and industry analysis, and review the footnotes to the statements.
- A low net worth or otherwise shaky financial statement increases the risk that the company may not be there for the long term.

ACTION PLAN

Find a good accountant by asking current franchisees and friends or contacts already in business who they use. Check the Yellow Pages or search for a local CPA at the American Institute of Certified Public Accountants Web site (www.aicpa.org).

THE TOP TEN WARNING SIGNS IN FRANCHISE INVESTMENTS

*C*HRIS WAS HAVING TROUBLE EVALUATING A RESTAURANT FRAN-
*chise. The company would not give her a UFOC, its
answers to her questions were confusing, and franchisees were giving a mixed review on some key issues. At
what point, she wondered, should she back away from the
program?*

DON'T GET SNAGGED

As exciting as it may be to purchase a franchise, this business requires all buyers to exercise CAUTION. Regulations require franchisors to give you a UFOC, that's all. Once you have this document in hand it is your responsibility to review it carefully, and to ask more questions of the franchisor and as many franchisees as you can.

KEY WARNING SIGNS

Even if you follow this advice, how do you know if there are problems with a franchise you have your eye on? Although there is no way to be absolutely certain about a given investment, you can improve your odds of success if you keep an eye out for some of these key warning signs:

10. *Weak Financial Statements.* The UFOC contains three years of the franchisor's audited financial statements. Review them carefully, and take them to a knowledgeable CPA. If the franchisor is in a weak financial condition, it will raise the risk levels for your investment. You may find some terrific programs being offered by thinly capitalized franchisors or start-up companies, but understand that your risks as a franchisee are magnified by the company's weak financial standing.

9. *No Answers.* If you do not get all of your questions answered by the franchisor, or if you start getting the feeling that the company is being evasive, move on.

8. *The Hustle.* Buying a franchise is a substantial investment. It might wipe out your life savings and put you on a financial bubble. If the seller is hurrying you along, telling you that the window of opportunity is closing, or using any other tried and true closing techniques, be prepared to walk away from the deal. This is too important to rush.

7. *Product Price Squeeze.* Product supply is the ticklish underbelly of franchise relationships. If you are buying a business that is designed to distribute the franchisor's product line, then you had better make sure the pricing of the product will allow you to be competitive in the marketplace. Ask other franchise owners how the pricing structure works for them. If you are going into a "business format" program where product is supplied by third parties, or some is supplied by the franchisor, make sure

that it runs well. Have the franchisees established a buying cooperative? Do franchisees have input on the supply arrangements? Make sure this key aspect of your business will not frustrate you.

6. *High Turnover Rates.* Check item 20 of the UFOC and confirm how many franchisees have left the system in the past three years. There is no rule of thumb to determine when the number is too high; this depends largely on the type of business. Lower-investment franchises generally have a higher turnover rate than more expensive businesses. If anything looks out of line, ask the franchisor what's going on.

5. *Attorney Avoidance.* The franchisor discourages you from getting a lawyer involved, telling you it will unnecessarily complicate and slow the process.

4. *Too Many Lawsuits.* Ours has become a litigious society, of course, and most franchisors reflect that fact. Item 3 of the UFOC will reveal the ten-year history of "material" lawsuits and/or arbitration cases filed against the company. If you see a heavy litigation history, find out what has been going on. Ask your attorney's opinion what they think. It could mean that franchisees are fundamentally unhappy in the business.

3. *Earnings Claims Mumbo Jumbo.* Ask the seller's representative: "How much money can I make with this franchise?" If it is not in the UFOC, the company must decline to answer the question. If they say, "We are prohibited by federal law from answering the question," realize that although that may be true, it may also be because the earnings picture is not a pretty one.

2. *No UFOC.* All franchisors are required by federal law and many state laws to deliver a UFOC before you pay any money for the franchise or sign a franchise agreement. If you do not receive one, don't even think about buying the franchised business.

And the number one warning sign in franchise investments:

1. *Consistently Bad Reports From Current Franchisees.* If you make the effort to visit with some current franchisees of the company, and each one tells you they are unhappy or would not make the investment in this franchise again, think long and hard about your own decision. There is no stronger or more trustworthy source of information about the company than those independents who are in the trenches. If they feel that the franchisor has let them down, or has a flawed program, it will tell you to look more carefully before you take the plunge.

These warning signs should prompt you to ask more questions. If you don't like the answers you receive, and your gut (or your professional advisor) tells you to head for the door, this is probably not the program for you. Take the time to look around at other programs. For a decision as important as this one, you owe it to yourself and your family to be confident that it is the right business investment for you.

SUMMARY NOTES

- Look for red flags indicating problems in the franchise program.
- The decision about whether or not to invest in a particular franchise is yours, and no one knows better than you what will fit with your needs. Carefully consider anything else that appears to be a red flag in your own judgment.

ACTION PLAN
Move on if you encounter any serious problems regarding a franchise that are not cleared up to your satisfaction.

CLOSING ON YOUR FRANCHISE PURCHASE

*N*OW IT WAS GETTING EXCITING FOR KEVIN. HE HAD GONE
*through all the steps with the franchisor, lined up
the financing he needed to develop the new business, and was ready to close the transaction. In just a few
days he would launch a new chapter of personal success
in his life. What did he need to know going into the closing meeting?*

Once the franchisor has thoroughly checked out the
applicant's qualifications, and the applicant has reviewed all
documents, seen an accountant and attorney, scraped
together the money necessary to buy the franchise, and
completed all necessary discussions, it is time to close on
the transaction.

Purchasing the franchise rights for a business that has not yet been built is not a complicated transaction, and the closing involves nothing more than signing a few contracts and sliding a check across the table for the initial franchise fee. Most "closings" for franchise sales do not take place in a room face to face with the franchisor. They take place through the mail. The company sends you a final package with tabs showing where your signature is needed and a cover letter stating the amount of the initial franchise fee. You sign and return, and it is done.

A CHECKLIST FOR CLOSING

However you should pay attention to the following before you sign on the dotted line:

The Franchise Agreement

This contract should have been in your hands with all blanks filled in for at least five business days before you sign and date it. That is a requirement imposed on the franchisor by state and federal law; it is not the franchisee's responsibility to see that this is met. Make sure your attorney has reviewed the contract and signed off on it. If you have requested any changes to be made to accommodate you, make sure they appear in the final form of the contract.

Many companies ask you to sign two originals and return them to the company. The franchisor then executes them and returns one original to you for your records.

Always Date Your Signature

Begin the habit of adding a date to any legal document that contains your signature. If the signature form does not have a space to show the date, simply jot it immediately after your signature. Dates are important in the regulation of franchise sales, and you may be called upon to swear as to a series of dated events. The date of delivery of the UFOC, the date you first had a face-to-face meeting with the franchisor, the date on which you received a completed franchise agreement, and the date on which you signed the franchise agreement, are all important.

Never backdate a document, even if asked to do so by the franchisor; it will only confuse your recollection of events. Make sure your document record is clear on the dates.

Other Contracts

You may be presented with other contracts to sign that are ancillary to the franchise agreement. All such documents should be included in the UFOC and not come as a surprise at closing. If you do receive a surprise contract, check it with your attorney. Ancillary contracts may include a site selection agreement (if you do not have a site selected yet), an agreement regarding necessary lease terms, and an acknowledgment of the training schedule.

UFOC

If you have not received the franchisor's UFOC at least ten business days before you are asked to sign the franchise agreement, stop. Don't sign the contract, and don't send any money. This could indicate a mere oversight, or it could mean that you have a more serious problem. Contact your franchisor representative.

Lease Paperwork

If you have selected a location for the franchised business, you probably have received a proposed lease from the landlord. Make sure that your attorney sees this lease form, and that you understand what requirements the franchisor might impose on the lease terms. It probably will not hold up the closing if this is not resolved, but you want to give all parties—and their attorneys—as much notice as possible regarding the potential terms of any lease.

Bank Paperwork

If you have arranged a loan from a bank or other lending institution, it will want to receive a copy of the franchise agreement (and every other piece of paper related to the franchise) as soon as possible. Talk to your banker about the steps necessary to provide the money you are borrowing, and when it will be available. Make sure all is in order before you close.

SUMMARY NOTES

- Prepare paperwork as you approach the closing.
- Prepare a checklist for the closing so that nothing is dropped. Confirm the list with your attorney.
- You should have checklist items for the contracts, the UFOC, your lease paperwork, and financing paperwork.

ACTION PLAN

Plan ahead so that you are sure of your costs and obligations before the closing. Meet with your attorney to consider all contingencies.

WHEN THINGS DON'T WORK OUT
RESOLVING FRANCHISOR/ FRANCHISEE LEGAL DISPUTES

*A*CCORDING TO *JEFF, "IT SEEMED LIKE A GOOD IDEA AT THE TIME."* *Jeff had carefully selected a franchise—an Italian Restaurant—and it would be the first and the best in his town. He found a strip mall location and threw his heart into it. He borrowed $350,000 and worked at the business 12 hours a day, seven days a week. He mopped floors after closing and managed the buying, hiring, and money. He personally welcomed his customers and spent a fortune on build-out and grand-opening advertising. Six months after the opening, the restaurant just wasn't cutting it, and Jeff was nearly out of operating cash. He stopped paying his royalties, telling the company that the program was not working in his town, and that he would pay the royalties as soon as the business made some money. Rather than come in to help, the franchisor sent a*

letter on lawyer's letterhead threatening termination for
failure to pay royalties if the account was not brought up
to date in 30 days.
"Now what do I do?" a bewildered Jeff asked.

The termination of a franchise agreement has been a legal flash point since the earliest days of franchising. Nowhere are the divergent interests of franchisors and franchisees brought into sharper focus, and no other feature of the franchise relationship has generated more disputes, arbitration, and litigation. When you combine the complexities of the typical franchise agreement, the regulation of franchise sales, the perception that big corporations (franchisors) are against the little guy (franchisees), and the substantial amounts of money invested, it presents a ready-made formula for legal disputes.

Attorneys are building lucrative careers helping franchisors and franchisees resolve these disputes. There are more than 2,000 members, including myself, of the Forum on Franchising of the American Bar Association, and the number is growing.

LINES OF DEFENSE: CONTRACT TERMS AND PROTECTIVE LAWS

Franchisees do have some tools however. The first is the franchise agreement.

The Contract

The first line of defense for the franchisee, and the fundamental legal guideline for any termination for the franchisor, is the franchise agreement. The contract spells out the conditions under which either party may terminate the relationship. Typically the franchisor will reserve the right to terminate on a series of grounds, some based on the franchisee's failure to cure a default after a written notice is delivered, and others based on incurable violations that lead to immediate or automatic termination.

If a termination occurs in violation of the terms of the franchise agreement, the franchisee has the right to bring a lawsuit against the franchisor under state law, seeking either a court order that the termination be stopped, or damages, or both.

State Relationship Laws

The franchise relationship laws are state laws that regulate terminations, nonrenewals, and some franchising practices. There are 19 U.S. jurisdictions that have adopted some form of franchise relationship law (see the list at Appendix A.) The typical relationship law requires that a franchisor have "good cause" before it moves to terminate a franchisee. This protects a franchisee from arbitrary or baseless terminations, and creates a right to sue the franchisor for damages if the standard is violated.

These laws were adopted in response to perceived widespread abuses in franchising. Unjust terminations and the absence of renewal rights seemed to be depriving franchisees of the value of the businesses they had built. Other abuses, such as no right of assignment, restricted right of association, unreasonable performance standards, and encroachment (placing another unit too close to a franchised unit), also led to the legislative attempt to level the playing field.

If the franchisee has an argument that a state relationship law supersedes the contract, there may be an opportunity to seek court relief under that law. The state relationship laws allow termination where the franchisor has "good cause" to terminate the franchise. What is "good cause"?

General Standard. Where the state law does define the concept, "good cause" means "failure of the franchisee to comply substantially with the requirements imposed by the franchisor." In other words, it means a breach of the franchise agreement.

Statutory Grounds. Here are some of the additional statutory grounds where termination is lawful:

- Voluntary abandonment.
- Criminal conviction of the franchisee on a charge related to the franchised business.
- The franchisee becomes insolvent or declares bankruptcy.
- Failure to pay the franchisor sums due.
- Loss of the right to occupy the franchisee's business premises.
- A material misrepresentation by the franchisee relating to the business.
- Franchisee conduct that materially impairs the goodwill of the franchised business or the franchisor's trademark.
- The franchisee's repeated noncompliance with the requirements of the franchise.
- Imminent danger to public health or safety.
- Failure to act in good faith and in a commercially reasonable manner.
- A written agreement to terminate.
- The franchisee's failure to comply with any law applicable to the operation of the franchise.
- Government seizure of the franchised business or foreclosure by a creditor.

DISPUTE RESOLUTION TOOLBOX

Obviously, there are lots of land mines on the path to franchise success. Given the strong interests and even stronger feelings among franchisors and franchisees over termination issues, resolving the inevitable disputes is something of an art form. As a franchisee you need to understand the tools in your dispute resolution toolbox.

There are four distinct types of dispute resolution tools, and each of them can be used in the franchise context.

IN*sight*

Franchise disputes can often be resolved if they are recognized and handled at an early moment in the dispute. Many franchisors express frustration that their contracts give them only one response to a serious problem— termination—and it is an atomic bomb. Mediation has become popular among franchisors and their lawyers as an effective technique for resolving business disputes without resorting to nuclear weaponry.

1. *Negotiation.* It has been said that negotiation and compromise are the oils that smooth the gears of business. Negotiation is the process of give and take that results in an acceptable solution for the parties involved. It takes a willingness to explore the possibilities with the other side, and benefits from face-to-face discussions.

What could our franchisee Jeff negotiate for in his situation? Perhaps he could seek a royalty concession until his business is on its feet, or propose to sign a promissory note for the amount of royalty owing with an installment repayment schedule. Or he could begin negotiations to either sell the business to a more aggressive owner or to the franchisor, or close the business with both parties working to minimize the financial impact on Jeff. The principal advantage of an effective negotiation is that it quickly embraces creative, business-oriented resolutions. With clever business people working in good faith, a negotiated resolution of a difficult situation offers the greatest hope for a solution that is fair to all involved.

2. *Mediation.* Mediation is professionally assisted negotiation. Where franchisor and franchisee are unable to negotiate a satisfactory solution, they may choose to bring into the discussion a

professional mediator. This is someone trained in the mediation process, and possibly experienced in the franchised business, who can use their skills to help the parties fashion a creative resolution. Often the most effective mediators are retired civil court judges. Mediation is nonbinding unless and until the parties find an agreeable solution; then they may commit to binding terms. Disputing parties can turn to the American Arbitration Association or national private organizations like JAMS for mediation services. Of particular interest to franchisors is the fact that a franchisor/franchisee dispute that is taken through a mediation process need not be disclosed in item 3 of the UFOC.

3. *Arbitration.* Arbitration is a more formal dispute resolution process that results in a final, nonappealable decision made by an arbitrator or a panel of three arbitrators. Think of arbitration as litigation without the courtroom. The result is just as binding on the parties as a court decision, and it must be disclosed in item 3 of the UFOC, just as court cases.

If your franchise agreement contains a provision that commits all disputes to binding arbitration, then you will not have the right to sue in a court of law. Except in rather extreme cases of fraud in the formation of the contract, the arbitration provision is almost always enforced by a court if challenged by one of the parties. The Federal Arbitration Act, and court decisions of the past 50 years, have created an extremely strong policy in favor of enforcing arbitration agreements. The policy reduces the crushing case load in our public courts, and allows private parties to resolve their disputes privately. It is not entirely private, however, because disputes submitted to arbitration must be disclosed in item 3 of the franchisor's UFOC.

4. *Litigation.* A franchisee can always sue a franchisor in court to enforce the terms of the franchise agreement, and try to stop a threatened termination. Of course, the franchisor can also sue to

enforce the payment requirements or other terms of the franchise agreement. Of all the dispute resolution tools available to franchisors and franchisees, litigation is by far the most expensive and time consuming.

After handling dozens of franchisor/franchisee disputes, I can assure you that one of your most important objectives in business is to avoid litigation, and to a lesser degree arbitration. Use these tools only as a last resort. It is a rare business owner who finds litigation satisfactory as a dispute resolution process.

SUMMARY NOTES

- In franchising, disputes happen.
- Your first line of defense as a franchisee is the franchise agreement. Look to the terms and conditions articulated in the contract, and ask your attorney for assistance.
- The second line of defense are specific standards adopted in the various franchise relationship laws.
- Dispute resolution techniques are important tools in your franchise business life. Familiarize yourself with the basic advantages and disadvantages of negotiation, mediation, arbitration, and litigation.

ACTION PLAN

Talk to your attorney about alternate forms of dispute resolution, and ask how dispute resolution is addressed in the contract. Discuss with the franchisor how you will both handle a dispute if and when it arises.

RENEWING YOUR FRANCHISE RIGHTS

*S*AM *REALIZED WITH A START ONE DAY THAT HIS FRANCHISE* agreement *was due to expire in a year.* "*Where has the time gone?*" *he thought. The foreseeable arrival of the expiration date means that Sam has some decisions to make. "Do I want to sign on for another five years? If I don't re-up, what will happen to my business? If I have a buyer for my business walk in tomorrow, what do I have to sell? What hoops do I have to jump through to renew the franchise rights? Will the renewal contract be on the same terms as my current contract?"*

CONTRACT TERMS AND RENEWAL RIGHTS

The franchise agreement is a long-term arrangement that can last more than 20 years. Many of the earliest

McDonald's franchise agreements from the 1960s and 1970s have completed their initial 20-year terms and have been renewed for another 20 years. I suspect some of those may even be coming around again.

Think of a franchise agreement as you would a lease for real estate. The lease/franchise agreement grants the tenant/franchisee the right to use the company's property (the building/franchise system) for a period of years and then, when the time is up, the relationship ends. The tenant/franchisee moves out and both parties go on their separate ways.

As with many commercial leases, the franchise agreement often grants the franchisee the conditional right to renew the relationship for another term of years, and the renewal right usually depends on meeting a short list of preconditions.

Before looking at those preconditions, it is necessary to understand the overall structure of the franchise agreement term. Current practice and conventional wisdom among franchisors suggest that you are not likely to find a full 20-year term granted at the outset of the relationship. Why? Because things change too much over such a long period of time. When circumstances change, or when the franchise system itself changes, the franchisor does not want to be locked into contracts that cannot keep up with these changes.

For instance, say that in its first 15 franchise agreements, a franchisor designated that the franchisee had an exclusive territory covering a radius of 30 miles from the store location. But then things change: the franchise system expands at an astonishing rate so there are lots of new locations, the company develops smaller, mobile locations for the service that can be flexible and nimble in following the market for the franchise product, the company develops a catalog to offer products directly to the customer, the company increases its standard royalty rate from 4 to 5 percent, the Internet is invented, and so on. The franchisor wants to be able to respond to such changes, so structures the franchise agreement to be for a five-year initial term with the option to renew for three additional terms of five years each.

The effect of such a multiterm structure is to allow the franchisor to present the franchisee with a new form of franchise agreement every five years, and each form can adapt the system to the current market circumstances. The franchisor wants to reduce the size of the exclusive territory and modify the concept of exclusivity. The franchisor can make those changes only if the terms of renewal allow the changes. The renewal also gives the franchisee a chance to evaluate the continuing value of participating in the franchise program. The franchisee can always walk away at the date of expiration. Today terms are shorter and there are more renewals than in the past. That's why contract renewal is an important topic for any franchisee looking at a new franchise agreement.

RENEWAL CONDITIONS

Renewal by the franchisee is typically articulated as a "right" or "option," but it always comes with conditions to be met. As with any legal contract, read the fine print to understand the steps necessary to satisfy the conditions and enjoy the full rights under the agreement.

What sorts of conditions will you encounter at renewal time? Here are the most common:

Give Written Notice to the Franchisor. This provision usually requires a written notice no less than x months and no more than y months prior to the date of expiration. It is designed this way so that renewal paperwork can be prepared and the franchisor can comply with state laws that may require a franchisor to give a certain amount of notice before failing to renew a franchise.

IN*sight*

Some franchise relationship laws (see Chapter 19 and Appendix A) require that a franchisor give at least 180 days notice to the franchisee of their intention not to renew a franchise agreement.

No Defaults and In Full Compliance. Look for a provision that says something like "You must not currently be in default under the franchise agreement, and must have remained in compliance during its term." What if you cured a minor default in your first year, are you in full compliance?

Sign a New Form of Franchise Agreement. This is the most sensitive of the renewal conditions. Does the contract allow the substitution of a new form of agreement and advise you that the terms of the renewal agreement may be substantially different from the current agreement? That allows the franchisor to increase your royalty rates, alter your grant of territorial protections, and change other features that might directly affect the value of your business. Some franchise agreements specify that royalty rates and territories will not be changed but that other provisions may be changed on renewal. This is a step in the right direction. Be sure to go over this provision with your attorney.

Sign a Release of Claims. Why does the franchisor require you to release legal claims as a condition of renewal? It has everything to do with the company's opportunity to cut off problems that might have occurred during the expiring term. This way, the franchisor can begin the new term on a new slate without concern that it will renew the contract and then get hit with a lawsuit over something that occurred in the earlier term. One idea that is usually acceptable to the franchisor: make the release mutual, so that the franchisor also releases any claims it may have against the franchisee under the expiring contract. Discuss this provision and any claims you may have under the current contract with your legal counsel.

Pay a Renewal Fee. In my experience a minority of franchise agreements require a renewal fee. Most don't, because franchisors generally want to impose no impediment to renewal. They want the franchisee to re-up. The franchisee represents an exceedingly valuable revenue stream for the franchisor, which would be expensive to replace if the franchisee did not renew.

Renewal is the strongest vote for the value of the franchise program that a franchisee can make. You will find that most franchisors generally want you to renew and will make renewal as easy and favorable as possible. A renewed franchise is far less expensive than finding, training, and establishing a new franchisee.

The answers to most of the questions Sam was pondering at the beginning of this chapter should be answered in his franchise agreement and by the renewal policies of the particular franchise system. Many of the franchise relationship laws discussed in Chapter 19 apply the "good cause" standard to a franchisor's failure to renew a franchise agreement and may therefore preempt the renewal terms laid out in your franchise agreement. Check with your attorney to consider any applicable statutory renewal standards.

SUMMARY NOTES

- Like a commercial lease, a franchise agreement typically grants a term of years with conditional renewal rights.
- The duration of franchise agreement terms is getting shorter. This offers flexibility to franchisor and franchisee alike.

- The conditions imposed on renewal may include notice, contract compliance, a new form of franchise agreement, a release of claims, and payment of a renewal fee.

ACTION PLAN

Keep these renewal concerns in mind when analyzing the initial franchise agreement. Ask the franchisor representative about renewal rights. Make sure your attorney is comfortable with the contract renewal language.

CHAPTER

21

INTERNATIONAL FRANCHISING

*E**NRIQUE LIVES IN MEXICO CITY, BUT HE HAS TRAVELED TO THE U.S. many times. He is excited about bringing an American restaurant concept to Mexico because his cosmopolitan city had never seen anything like it. Enrique contacted the franchisor in Minneapolis thinking it was a long shot, and was surprised to find that the company has an active international franchising department with a Spanish-speaking specialist in Latin America. Things are looking up for Enrique.*

THE GLOBALIZATION OF FRANCHISING

The global expansion of U.S. franchisors is one of the most interesting business success stories in the past 30 years. The American franchise concept has dispersed its various familiar brand names in large and small countries around the world at an astonishing rate.

McDonald's restaurants has been a global franchise expansion leader. It has established 28,000 restaurants in more than 120 countries, recently announcing new restaurant locations in French Guiana and San Marino. The company says that 80 percent of its restaurants worldwide are franchised. The Holiday Inn group, a leading franchisor of Holiday Inn hotels and other brands, has opened hotels in nearly 100 countries.

IN*sight*

The history of international franchise expansion has not been—as they say in the United Kingdom—all beer and skittles. In the 1980s, McDonald's restaurants reported enormous difficulties in establishing their foods supply organization in foreign locations like Russia and Asia. Other franchisors have had their international expansion plans frustrated at huge expense by national laws restricting money transfer, trademark pirates and poorly enforced intellectual property laws, poor reception of their products because of cultural concerns, and communications problems.

Franchise regulation has been growing as well. The countries with a form of presale disclosure requirements for franchisors include Australia, Brazil, Canada (Ontario and Alberta), China, France, Indonesia, Italy, Japan, Malaysia, Mexico, South Africa, South Korea, Spain, and the United States. Buy a franchise in one of these countries and you will likely receive a pre-sale disclosure statement presenting some of the key information you will need to evaluate the proposed franchise investment.

KEYS TO FOREIGN-BASED FRANCHISES

The international expansion of franchising has now come full circle as franchisors from other lands expand into the U.S. market. If you are interested in purchasing an international franchise, located in the U.S. market or another country, make sure you consider the following:

Find out if the company has taken steps to comply with all of the laws on franchising in this country. Does the company have a UFOC or other disclosure statement? Is it complete? Has the company registered its offering in the U.S. registration states? If it has complied with these laws, that tells you the company has made a substantial investment in seeking successful franchisees in the U.S. market. If it has sidestepped these requirements, it is trying to cut some important corners, and you should be careful. You could be the next corner.

Is the program a regional offering or limited to one market? Will you receive rights for several markets or multiple states? Many companies new to the U.S. market divide up the country into separate, multistate regions so that penetrating such a huge commercial country is manageable.

How is the U.S. expansion going to be managed? Is there a regional manager or master franchisee? Make sure you understand how the relationships are set up so that you know who will provide things like training and services. This may not be clear after you review the UFOC, so plan to discuss it with the sales representatives you meet.

One of the largest challenges of international franchising is effective communication. Will the company be communicating directly with the U.S. franchisees, or will it go through its regional managers/master franchisees? Find out if regular meetings will be held, and where. If they are overseas, be sure that you include these costs in your budgeting. Ask if the franchisor will assist with any meeting expenses.

Trademark protection can be a challenge for a franchisor from outside the United States. Be sure to check item 13 of the UFOC describing the U.S. registration status of the principal trademark. If it is not registered with the U.S. Patent and Trademark Office, exercise extreme caution and have your attorney check it out.

Is the cultural fit of the business a good one? Has the product/service been tested in the U.S. market, or are you the test? If you are the pioneer for this program, make sure you will not be too badly hurt if the product/service flops. It does happen. And it will happen regardless of the level of your enthusiasm and industry. Make sure your lawyer takes steps to protect you in the event the project goes south.

Don't shy away from an opportunity just because it is a franchisor from another country. The UFOC will tell you a lot about the company and how it is organized to service the U.S. market. Ask for the UFOC early on. If it does not exist, always proceed with extreme caution.

SUMMARY NOTES

- An international franchise can make an exciting investment, and more and more foreign-based franchisors tackle the U.S. market.
- Protect yourself by looking into the three key areas of an international relationship: control, communication, and commitment.
- Find out how the market will be managed. Is there a regional manager or U.S. master franchisee, or will the company manage its franchisees directly?
- Make sure that the program will be successful in the U.S. market. Foreign success does not always translate to the U.S. market.

ACTION PLAN

Contact and meet with managers responsible for franchising an international brand in your area. Locate other franchisees of the system in your area.

PART IV

THE BUSINESS
OF BUSINESS OWNERSHIP

NEGOTIATING FRANCHISE AGREEMENTS AND BUSINESS OPPORTUNITY CONTRACTS

*M*ARIA DISLIKES BUYING CARS FOR ONE REASON: SHE HATES *having to negotiate aggressively on the price to get a fair deal. Now that she is buying a business opportunity she has the same feeling as she gets closer to closing the transaction. Is it supposed to be like buying a car? Is she expected to negotiate? Maria wonders if she has enough information to negotiate on this purchase but remembers her dad always saying, "Everything is negotiable."*

The purchase of a franchise can be an intimidating process. Most Americans have never seen, let alone signed, a contract of such length and complexity as a typical business format franchise agreement. Signing one under any circumstances takes an act of courage and a leap of faith.

Buying a business opportunity is generally not as complex or expensive, but it can be just as intimidating. Maria wonders if it's like buying a car because she has never bought a business opportunity before and doesn't know the ropes.

The lesson that Maria's dad taught her is always true in business, and it applies with equal force to franchises and business opportunities. Don't miss the opportunity to negotiate your purchase.

NEGOTIATING A BUSINESS OPPORTUNITY

The best leverage point in your negotiation of a business opportunity is your willingness to walk away from the deal if you can't buy it on your terms. This statement is generally true in all of your business dealings. Offer to pay a lower price. Offset some of your risk by deferring some or all of the purchase price until goods or services are delivered by the seller. Propose a payment schedule over six months. Ask for a lower price if you pay cash. Most business opportunity sellers are not price sensitive, even though they often present their program as being deeply discounted for an immediate purchase. Use some of the techniques discussed in this chapter, and you could save yourself hundreds of dollars.

NEGOTIATING A FRANCHISE AGREEMENT

Signing a franchise agreement comes at the end of a lengthy process, highlighted by the delivery of a UFOC, promotional brochures, other system literature, and personal interviews. Pressing for favorable contract terms may be the last thought on your mind. However, with some planning and understanding of the franchisor's position, you can cut a far better legal and financial deal.

WHY IS THE FRANCHISE AGREEMENT SO ONE SIDED?

Franchise agreements have always been weighted in the franchisor's favor for one simple reason: the franchisor is not only your partner in this venture, it is the system-wide enforcer. It is in everyone's interests—the franchisor's, yours, and other franchisees'—that all franchisees operate in a manner that meets the highest system standards. In a retail system, all stores must be clean and well run. If the store closest to you is dirty, slow, or run down it affects your business directly and dramatically. Both units operate under the same trademark; if your neighbor is injuring the local reputation of the mark, you pay the price. Customers who have visited the dirty store will naturally assume that your store is in the same condition, and stay away in droves. To paraphrase the great Yogi Berra, "If people don't want to come to your store, how are you going to stop them?"

As the system standards enforcer, the franchisor must reserve draconian enforcement rights in the franchise agreement. These may strike you as overbearing, but they are designed to allow the franchisor to take action if a franchisee's operation is subpar. In a sense, the enforcement provisions are there to protect you as well. When your neighbor's careless operation starts to hurt your business, you will be the first one to request that the franchisor do something to correct the situation. The franchisor had better have tough enforcement provisions in the franchise agreement or they will be powerless to do anything. Negotiating some of these provisions will be tough.

UNDERSTANDING THE SELLER'S POSITION

Powerful financial forces drive the franchisor to complete the franchise transaction. It is difficult, time consuming, and expensive for a franchisor to locate a qualified franchisee. Selling a franchise is the ultimate hard sell; the sales cycle is measured in months, not days. Most franchisors devote tens of thousands of dollars a year to recruiting franchisees, and once a qualified applicant shows an interest the franchisor is *highly* motivated to complete the sale. A new franchisee in the system means a stream of revenue that will last for years and continued growth for the system.

Franchise sales representatives, like business opportunity seller representatives, are often paid in whole or in part on commission. They are extremely motivated to see the transaction close; if you walk away, they lose money.

The point is that you are in a position of considerable power when it comes to negotiating a franchise agreement. Use that power to your advantage.

IN*sight*

The power of your position is expressed in your attitude: you are interested in buying but not overeager. You let the seller know that you are interested, but there are lots of other investments you are evaluating (even if in your heart you know this is the one). Negotiation expert Herb Cohen says the best negotiating attitude says to the other side: "I care about making this commitment, but not that much."

TAKE IT OR LEAVE IT?

How easy is it to negotiate the terms of a franchise agreement? While it complicates the life of franchisors, it is a well-known secret in the franchisor community that these contracts are negotiated all the time. You may hear from a franchisor that franchise law prohibits negotiation (it doesn't), or the company does not want to negotiate the terms that are offered to you, but you should not understand that to mean that the company *cannot* change its contract for you.

In fact, even the law of California—the toughest jurisdiction on negotiated changes in a franchise offering—allows franchisors to negotiate the terms of a franchise, but imposes a series of disclosure and registration obligations on a franchisor who changes the terms of its standard, registered offer. At the other end of the legal spectrum, the franchise law in the Commonwealth of Virginia states that a franchise agreement may be voided by the franchisee within a short time if it is *not* negotiated by the franchisor.

A franchisor can change the standard contract terms for you if it chooses to make the changes.

NEGOTIATING RULES

Steven B. Wiley, founder of the Wiley Group in Gettysburg, Pennsylvania, and one of the country's leading motivators and instructors of top corporate executives in matters of building partnerships and negotiating techniques, has some key suggestions for your negotiation. "First, there is no substitute for doing your homework," says Wiley. "Talk to other franchisees and find out where the company has shown flexibility in the past, talk to an experienced franchise lawyer, ask the franchisor for as much background information as you can. When you meet with the company to talk about the terms of the franchise agreement,

---

IN*sight*

Check item 5 of the UFOC ("Initial Franchise Fee"). If the initial franchise fee is not uniform, the company is required to disclose a formula or the actual initial fees paid in the prior fiscal year. If the company cut some deals on the initial franchise fee, they will be at least mentioned here.

---

you want to know as much as you can about that contract. You will be prepared, and you will not be thrown off balance when the give and take starts."

Keep in mind that you are about to commence a long-term business relationship with the franchisor. It is in your and the franchisor's interests that both parties are happy with the deal struck and comfortable with any changes you agree to make. If you are not happy with any aspect of the contract, or there is a provision that you do not understand, you need to make your position known to the franchisor representatives.

According to Steve Wiley, the number-one negotiating principle to keep in mind is to "start high." "I teach corporate managers at the largest companies in the world that they need to start with an aggressive opening position," says Wiley. "Not because they should be greedy, rather it is so that they can make concessions along the way of the discussion and work toward their target position. If you open at what you consider a fair position you will have no room to maneuver when the other side asks you for something."

A prospective franchisee negotiating the franchise agreement should always be prepared to walk away from the deal. "This is the real strength of any negotiator," says Wiley. "Your neutral attitude says to the other side that you are not overeager to conclude the deal, that you want the deal but only if it is on reasonable terms. Even if you think this is the opportunity of a lifetime that will make you wealthy beyond your wildest dreams, never show it to the other side or you will not conclude the deal on your terms."

FRANCHISORS' INFLEXIBLE POSITIONS

Many provisions of the franchise agreement can be negotiated, but there are a few areas where franchisors can be expected to dig in their heels:

Trademarks

As the owner of the trademarks, a franchisor will not be at all willing to water down their legal rights to control the display of the mark or protect the mark through enforcement actions. There is usually some wiggle room in the degree to which a franchisor is willing to stand behind the mark if the franchisee is attacked legally for its use of the mark. Look for language by which the company "indemnifies" (will pay) the franchisee for legal expenses incurred where the franchisee has properly used the marks and finds themselves under legal attack by someone claiming infringement.

Royalty Rates

Conventional wisdom in the franchisor community suggests that all franchisees should pay the same rate of royalty whenever possible. This keeps everyone in the system on the same footing and avoids creating different classes of franchise citizens in the system. So if the standard royalty rate is set at 5 percent, don't expect the company to accept your suggestion that you pay a royalty rate of 4 percent.

There may be extenuating circumstances where you would be allowed to pay a lower rate for a period of time, but those are relatively rare. If you are taking over a store that has been poorly managed and the customer base is depleted, you may want to suggest a break in the royalty rate for your first year while you turn around the operation.

Assignment/Termination Controls

Franchisors will do their best to exercise control over the people who are allowed to own and operate their franchises. They have a direct interest; all those franchises are flying a flag owned by the company. If a weak operator is allowed to come in through a sale, or someone comes in who does not have the capital to run the business successfully, it creates a threat of business failure. That hurts the reputation of the system and indirectly all franchisees.

If an operator is not following the program or their operations are not clean or they are otherwise hurting the system's reputation, the company has little choice but to take corrective steps. For these reasons, franchisors are not likely to give on suggested changes to the assignment or termination provisions.

FRANCHISORS' FLEXIBLE POSITIONS

Franchisors tends to have more flexibility in other areas of the contract:

Initial Fee

The franchisor has great flexibility when it comes to the initial fee. If it is set at $30,000, you may be able to argue for a reduction of that amount or a plan by which you defer payment over time. Try suggesting that you pay $15,000 upfront and the balance over the first 18 months of your operation of the business.

There may be some resistance to this concept, of course. Perhaps the company needs the upfront fee to pay a commission to the broker or for its own operating expenses. Franchisors are also reluctant to make any changes that require additional disclosure. If there are variations in the initial fee, the company may have to disclose that fact in item 5 of its UFOC. If the company offers financing, it may be required to disclose those terms as well as in item 10. Ask anyway; it's your money, after all.

Territorial Rights

This is ticklish in some systems, but well worth exploring in negotiations. What are the dimensions of the territory you are granted? Can you request an expansion of that area or ask for an option right on an adjoining territory? Perhaps you could request additional time and territorial protection during the first few years of your franchise. It may take a bit of creativity on your part, but it is well worth exploring if there are ways that you can structure the territorial rights to your own needs.

Marketing Contributions

This topic, and the franchisor's flexibility on it, will be determined by the type and the circumstances of the business. You may suggest that a local marketing fee be waived because of the unusual location: If you are building a retail store on the grounds of a popular theme park, you should not be paying marketing fees to increase foot traffic to your location. Your rent rate may be higher precisely because you have a premium location where foot traffic is delivered by the park's own promotion.

Never forget the fundamental impulse of good negotiators: it never hurts to ask. Build a win-win franchise agreement going in, and your relationship will be that much stronger for the long term.

SUMMARY NOTES

- Get creative when buying a franchise or business opportunity. Propose price reductions and payment terms that fit your needs.
- When you first read a franchise agreement it may strike you as one sided. But there are reasons for that. There are other players here; this is not merely a two-party agreement.
- Position yourself for negotiation. Gather as much information as you can about deals the franchisor has granted to others.
- It's legal in all states to negotiate a franchise agreement.
- Remember some of the key rules of negotiation: do your homework; "start high," be willing to walk on the deal, and "it never hurts to ask."
- There are some areas (initial fees, territory, advertising contributions) where a franchisor is more likely to give than other areas (trademark, royalties, and transfer rights).

ACTION PLAN

Become a good negotiator. Take a seminar on negotiation skills, or head to the library or bookstore for a book on negotiation, such as the classic You Can Negotiate Anything *by Herb Cohen (Bantam Books).*

WORKING WITH LAWYERS AND ACCOUNTANTS

*B*OBBY IS A PRO AT COACHING HIGH SCHOOL KIDS, BUT IS LOST *when it comes to reading a balance sheet or under-standing dense legal language in a contract. He had what he considered an excellent franchise investment opportunity, but knew he needed some professional help. Could he afford it? Could he afford not to get help?*

USING LEGAL SERVICES

Anyone buying a franchise today is well advised to retain the services of an experienced attorney to review the franchise agreement and any related contracts. Business opportunity buyers, depending on the size of the invest-ment, may need an attorney's help as well. The objection is right on the tip of your tongue, isn't it? "How can I afford a lawyer? I am putting this business together on a shoestring as it is. A lawyer's going to cost me a fortune."

In the first place, using the services of an attorney need not cost a fortune, and you can work out in advance what fees are likely to be involved. Most lawyers still charge for their services by the hour, but many are willing to set a quoted fee or agree to a cap on the fee for a simple project like the review of a franchise agreement and UFOC. If it takes a lawyer two hours to review the document and another hour to meet with you to discuss it, that suggests a legal fee—assuming a $150 hourly rate—that does not exceed $500. Hiring an attorney is like buying insurance. And as insurance goes, $500 is not expensive at all. You can expect to purchase casualty insurance, health coverage for your employees, and unemployment compensation insurance that will put the cost of your modest attorney fees to shame.

IN*sight*

Attorneys know their clients are concerned about legal fees, and generally encourage discussion of the subject at the first meeting. Gone are the days when attorneys thought it unprofessional to discuss money.

What can you expect to receive for your legal fees? At a minimum you want to hear from your learned counsel whether there are any provisions in the proposed contract that run distinctly against your interests. You also want to know about provisions that put your investment in a precarious position. For instance, what if the franchisor reserves the right to terminate the relationship with no advance notice if you fail to follow the standards in the operating manuals? Your lawyer should advise you that this is way too broad and threatens your business in an unacceptable manner. They may suggest that language be added that gives you the right to receive at least 30 days' written notice of the infraction and an opportunity to cure it without threatening your entire investment in the program.

You also want to hear from your lawyer if there are any other aspects of the franchise documents that cause concern or call for further investigation. If you live in one of the several states requiring a franchisor to register under a franchise law or file for an exemption under a state business opportunity law, your lawyer should make the phone call to check on the company's status. Ask your attorney to tell you if your state's law protects you from an arbitrary or groundless termination by the franchisor. They should be able to give you a copy of any such law.

Do You Need a Specialist?

In this age of professional specialization, how do you find a lawyer experienced enough to be of help reviewing a franchise agreement? Referrals are by far the most effective way to locate the right lawyer. As you meet franchise owners in the system you are investigating, ask them who they use. Every state has a lawyer referral system you can look up in your phone book. Ask your friends and business acquaintances for referrals. You don't want the name of a cousin's brother-in-law who just graduated from law school in another state, but you do want to hear about lawyers a person has used and knows are experienced. Get familiar with the *Martindale-Hubbell Law Directory*, available in every law library and most public libraries, and online (www.martindale.com). This directory lists lawyers by state and town, and many entries include a short description of their professional background. It even offers a rating system of lawyers.

USING ACCOUNTING SERVICES

The other professional assistance you should consider hiring is a competent accountant. Accountants are worth their weight in Big Mac sandwiches if you are planning to go into business and are evaluating a franchise or business opportunity investment.

First and foremost, your accountant can put together a detailed projection for your business and help you consider how to finance the total investment. The projection will tell you a lot about the business. It should show where your break-even points will be, the number of customers you will need in order to generate your revenue, and the amount of your investment plus financing costs. It will also give you an idea of the return you can expect on your investment.

In short, your accountant can help you decide whether you would be better off financially buying the franchise or business opportunity or getting a job and putting your money in treasury bonds.

Your accountant can also look over the franchisor's three years of audited financial statements contained in the UFOC. These tell you a lot about the staying power of the company. Will it be there for the long haul? Do the statements show healthy growth or stagnating losses? Your accountant should be able to provide a professional opinion about the standing of the franchisor.

A full review by a CPA can be expensive, running into a few thousand dollars rather quickly. Talk to your accountant about what you need and what it's going to cost. Then figure out a way to do it.

WHAT TO ASK YOUR LEGAL AND ACCOUNTING ADVISORS

Some Great Questions for Your Attorney

Plan to explore these basic topics with your attorney, and add to the list whatever you think is appropriate for the franchise or business opportunity your are reviewing:

- How does this franchise agreement compare to others you have reviewed?

- Are there any provisions in this agreement that I should not agree to under any circumstances ("deal breakers")? Do you have any suggested changes for the agreement, and would they be accepted by the franchisor?

- Have you checked with state authorities to confirm that the company is registered to sell franchises or business opportunities in this state?

- How do the termination provisions stack up under this state's franchise laws or case law on termination? What exactly are my transfer rights under the agreement?

- Do any of the litigation or arbitration cases disclosed in item 3 concern you?

- What protections do I need when buying this business opportunity? Should I defer payments or otherwise structure the transaction? Are there any surety bonds, escrow arrangements, or trust accounts in place in this state to protect buyers of this program?

Some Great Questions for Your Accountant/CPA

- What is the seller's net worth? How does this amount relate to the size of my total investment in the franchise? Should I be concerned about it?

- Can you tell from the financial statement whether the seller's business is profitable? How would you describe the seller's financial health?

- Does the financial statement show the average annual royalty payment received from a franchisee? Can we extrapolate any average sales figures from that?

- Is there a surety bond, escrow account, or deferred payment in place in this state? Is there another entity that guarantees the obligations of the seller for this program?
- How do the item 7 figures strike you compared to other small businesses you have advised? Do they look reasonable?
- What is the break-even point for this business? What revenues will I need to cover my expenses and make the franchise or business opportunity profitable?

SUMMARY NOTES

- Ask franchisees you meet who they use for legal services. Do your research and find a good lawyer with experience representing small businesses.
- Think of legal and accounting expenses as part of your insurance costs.
- Get organized in your use of legal and accounting services. Know what questions you want answered in the preliminary review process.

ACTION PLAN

Interview a few attorneys and accountants to see their individual styles, experience, and capabilities. Be sure to confirm in advance that you will not be billed for the interview.

QUESTIONS FOR FRANCHISEES AND BUSINESS OPPORTUNITY OWNERS

*N*ANCY KNEW SHE NEEDED TO TALK TO SOME FRANCHISEES IN *the ham store business she was investigating, but was a bit intimidated. Was she imposing on them? Would she offend these experienced business people with her intrusive call? What would she say?*

THE KEY TO YOUR RESEARCH

Current franchisees and business opportunity owners are without a doubt the best source of information you will find on the benefits, drawbacks, and strengths of the business you are investigating. They can also generally provide some great insights and advice. It takes a bit of gumption to approach a business owner, but you should not hesitate. Here are some thoughts on the approach.

First, check out the business as a customer. If it is a retail operation, go to the unit, sit for a while, and observe the operation. Return to do this again during different times of the day. Learn to be a keen observer on these visits: count customers as they come in the door, observe how the employees handle their jobs (what do they say at the counter when they greet a customer?), note the amount of the purchases made by customers to get a rough estimate of the "average ticket" spent in the store, and observe what you can of the work going on out back.

The next step is to make arrangements to talk to the owner. Remember that retail business owners are extremely busy at certain times of the day. It's best to call ahead and find a good time to visit. When the owner does meet with you, be sensitive to the time you spend. If you requested a 20-minute interview, stick to it. If it is a busy lunch hour at a restaurant, you may want to find a better time of day.

FRANCHISE QUESTIONS

It also helps to have a set of questions prepared. Don't try to wing it. Here is a checklist of franchise questions to ask:

- Is the training program worthwhile? Did it leave you well prepared to run this business?
- Has the franchisor's support been steady? Are they there when you need them?
- What is the culture of the franchise system? Are franchisees friendly with one another? Is it encouraging or discouraging to be with the franchisor?
- Is the business seasonal? What are the strongest and weakest times of the year?
- Does the franchisor provide continuing training?
- Is the market for this business a strong one? Is it growing or slowing?

- Is there a franchisee association or council? Do franchisees have a real role in the franchisor's decision-making process?
- Did you have a good year last year? Do you recall what your gross sales were? Will this year be stronger or weaker?
- How is product supply arranged for franchisees? Does it work well?
- What questions do you wish you had asked going into your franchise investment?
- Knowing what you now know, would you buy this franchise again?

INsight

Most franchise owners will discuss the performance of their business once you establish a rapport with them. They need to know you are not a competitor or potential competitor but someone serious about making the same investment decision they made.
Most want to help.

BUSINESS OPPORTUNITY QUESTIONS

Here are a few business opportunity questions that could come in handy:

- How long ago did you purchase your business opportunity? Has it worked well for you?
- Did the seller do everything they said they would?
- Have you recouped your original investment? Have you lost or made money? How much did you make with this program last year (gross *and* net)?

- Were there any questions you wished you had asked the seller when you first became involved in this business?
- Were the materials in this business opportunity package done well? Could you understand this business from the materials, or did it take training, or a lot of trial and error on the job?
- Knowing what you now know, would you buy this business opportunity again?

Don't hesitate to take notes during your conversations. It tells the franchisee or business opportunity owner you value their words and experience. And resist the urge to get too chatty or argumentative. Your objective is to gather information. If you hear comments that concern you, by all means follow up with the seller's representative.

SUMMARY NOTES

- When approaching a franchisee, be respectful of time and business demands.
- Visit the business as a customer.
- Prepare a set of questions to discuss. Don't wing it.
- Take notes, and follow up with the franchisor if you hear answers that concern you.

ACTION PLAN

Create a list of owner questions for each franchise or business opportunity you investigate. Make full notes after each interview and drop them in your file.

SKILL SETS OF THE SUCCESSFUL FRANCHISEE AND BUSINESS OPPORTUNITY OWNER

*C*AROLYN PLANS TO BUY A RETAIL BUSINESS BECAUSE SHE HAS *always dreamed about having a stream of customers whom she pleases with scrumptious teas, cakes, and other treats. She enjoys meeting her customers face to face and looks forward to owning her own shop. She wonders what else she will need to know to be successful. Are there skills that she could learn that will help in her business?*

Carolyn is asking the right questions because all successful small business owners develop a distinct skill set. At the heart of any franchised business or business opportunity are some basic elements of business operation and business development that must be mastered. Falter on these basics and your business may have some serious problems. The most success-ful business owners develop these skill sets and drill them into their employees.

THE ART OF THE SALE

Business is selling. All businesses boil down quickly to this realiza-tion; franchises and business opportunities are no exception. It does not matter whether you are a junior manager in the world's largest organi-zation or the owner of your own small business, the engine of both busi-nesses is driven by sales activity.

Remember this basic truth of business: "Nothing happens in busi-ness until someone, somewhere makes a sale."

It follows that your key to success is to become a student of the sale; become an expert in the process and the techniques used by the best salespeople. Try to learn the basic rules for presenting features and benefits, overcoming objections, and closing techniques. Park yourself in the business book section of your local library and crawl through a few books on selling. There are dozens of titles available. Drink them in.

COUNTER MAGIC

One of the most fascinating aspects of retail business is the study of what happens at the counter, that magic place where the front-line rep-resentatives of your business meet your customers. When I say the "counter" of your business, I mean it literally and metaphorically. All busi-nesses meet customers, whether it is on the telephone, over the Internet, or at the customer's residence or place of business. In a tradi-tional retail business, it will literally be a countertop at your location.

Successful franchise organizations have pioneered and perfected the techniques at the counter that can have enormous payoffs in business.

No one has taught us more than the great Ray Kroc of McDonald's restaurants. He insisted that counter workers greet all customers with a smile and a cheery "Welcome to McDonald's!" The company reinforced the message with advertising showing the warm smiles of perky counter people welcoming you to McDonald's. "We love to see you smile."

Kroc also drove billions of dollars in sales, and propelled his organization to prominence, by teaching all counter people to say six simple words to every customer: "Would you like fries with that?" The resulting sales figures changed the landscape of American business.

IN*sight*

Pete and Laura Wakeman, founders of Great Harvest Bread Co., the largest whole-wheat bakery franchise in the United States, developed an entire marketing program, based on their teachings of what should happen at the customer counter, that is vital to all Great Harvest bakeries today. Their counter techniques teach franchisees and their employees the value of smiling and generosity of spirit, and ways to personally connect with the customer.

Whatever franchised business you manage, study what is happening at the counter. Put your training resources to work on the exchange. Make sure your employees follow your example and stick to your counter procedures. Study and watch their performance and try new ideas. Keep your counter fresh, enthusiastic, and fun, and your customers will come back time and again for more.

YOUR PROFITS ARE IN THE DETAILS

One thundering lesson of business ownership is just how small is the portion of gross revenue that actually falls into your pocket as profit. These small "margins" can represent vast fortunes, of course, when a business is run on a modestly large scale. Even at a large scale, though, the details determine whether the business comes out on the profitable side of the small margins or on the loss side of the profit/loss measure.

You have no choice but to become a student of the details of your franchised business. A few cents break on the price of your wholesale inventory, the lower costs of office supplies when purchased in bulk, the small incremental costs of condiments, managing the costs of labor— these details make all the difference.

BECOME A BEAN COUNTER

Money is the language of business, and accountants are the interpreters of the language. As a business owner you must master the language and become conversant in balance sheets and monthly operations statements. If problems are brewing in your business, they will show up first in the monthly numbers. You will get to know intimately your percentages of food costs, labor, administrative costs, and gross profit. This takes some study, so cozy up to your favorite accountant and tell them that you think this is the beginning of a beautiful friendship.

BE A SKILLED NEGOTIATOR

It often surprises people coming from a job into business ownership just how much of small business dealings are subject to a fluid marketplace, where prices and terms are determined by the give and take of negotiation. It takes a spot of courage to ask for a better price or payment terms or faster delivery, but it gives you the edge you need in your business. Your suppliers and business customers expect many aspects of

In all negotiations know beforehand how low you will go before you stop negotiating, and what you consider your target. When opening your discussion, "start high" and then be prepared to make concessions as the other side (starting low) pulls you down toward your target endpoint. Asking for more than you will settle for will not insult anyone. It will leave you some room to make concessions to the other side. That will put you in the give and take of business—right where you need to be.

the sale to be negotiated, so be prepared to jump in. Review the negotiating principles outlined in Chapter 22.

PEOPLE MANAGEMENT

Small business ownership is little more than the management of employees. Keep them happy, well paid, and motivated, and your business will be on solid ground. Give no personal attention, underpay, and discourage them with a punishing attitude, and you will experience high turnover and low productivity. Given typically low margins in small businesses, this can make the difference between a profitable business and a troubled one.

BUILD AN ORGANIZATION

It's been said that the owner does not build a business; they build an organization of people and the organization builds the business. Think about building a team of talented people, look for the best you can find, and try to stay out of their way as they build your business.

BE AN A+ FRANCHISEE

If your business is a franchise, follow the rules of the system. Part of being a top-performing franchised business is full and careful compliance with all aspects of the franchise program. That means paying royalties on time, showing up for meetings, and taking educational opportunities as they come along. Be a leader among franchise owners who do their best to promote the brand. Not only is this good business, it will add to the value of your business and may open opportunities down the road for expansion. The franchisor will naturally look to its A+ franchisees when new opportunities present themselves.

COLLECTING MONEY

The biggest challenge you face as a small business owner is the collection of money owed to you. For all businesses, successful collection is a combination of smart routine business practice and persistence.

When do you know you have a collection problem? Here are the symptoms:

- An unacceptably high level of accounts receivable.
- No office policy on collections.
- Too many bad checks.
- No information on the customer who pays on credit (including by check!).
- An inability to be decisive and move promptly against the deadbeat.
- No way to recover the expenses associated with debt collection, such as attorney's fees, interest, and late charges.

No one likes collection problems. If you are new to business, the reluctance of your customers to pay their bills can be a surprise. After all, you have always paid your mortgage, utility bills, credit card statements, and household expenses on time. Why can't your customers do the same?

Often the reason they do not pay in a timely fashion is *you*. Your routine credit extension practices, the information you gather on your customers, and the way you respond to slow payment all dictate the success you have at getting paid.

The best advice is to create a *written policy statement* that details exactly how credit will be extended or how a new customer account will be set up. Give a copy of the policy to the customer. The policy should spell out all credit procedures and collection policies. For your internal use, develop form letters that you use when a customer is late, and prepare to respond immediately.

Use some form of credit application that gathers this basic information about the account: name, address, telephone number (work and residence), social security number (this is essential), place of employment, bank account information, and property ownership information (automobiles and homes). If you are extending credit to a corporation, be sure to obtain the formal corporate name, the date and state of incorporation, and the employer identification number. Without this basic information, collections can be a nightmare. The following are some tips for smart collection practices:

Don't Accept Bad Checks. Examine all checks carefully. A quick way to spot a forged check is to look for the perforations. *Most forged checks are produced on plain paper stock with no perforated edges.* Real check paper stock allows the check to be removed from a perforated edge. Bank tellers are trained to look for this distinctive feature.

Is the date correct? If the date is old (generally more than three or four weeks) or if it has been postdated, do not accept it.

Is the amount properly stated? Does the numerical figure agree with the written dollar amount? *If the number, the written amount, or the payee (you) is illegible, written over, or hard to read in any way, do not take the check.*

Be careful accepting a two-party check. A two-party check is made to one person, and that person offers to endorse the check to you. Unless you know both parties, you run a risk that the original maker will stop payment on the check.

Look out for checks that show a *low sequence number.* This indicates a recently opened account since most banks begin numbering a new checking account at #101. Just be more cautious when the number is low.

Do Not Put Off Collecting on the Debt. *The longer you wait to take action, the more difficult it will be to collect on an overdue account.* An account receivable that is more than 90 days old should be turned over for collection, either to a collection agency, who will handle the matter for a hefty percentage of the outstanding bill, or to your attorney.

Use a Credit Agreement. You cannot collect interest, late fees, or attorney's fees without the written agreement of the customer. A credit agreement also spells out the terms of the credit being extended and shows you take this account, the credit, and collections *seriously.*

SUMMARY NOTES

- Running your business is the ultimate challenge. Brush up on the skills that are essential to all business operations: master the art of the sale, manage details, count beans, negotiate, manage people effectively, build an organization, be an A+ franchisee, and collect the money you are owed.

ACTION PLAN

Take a course at a local college, university, or business school to learn more about areas of business that are mystifying to you.

MAKE IT HAPPEN

*S*EAN HAS TOYED WITH THE IDEA OF STARTING HIS OWN BUSINESS *for more than five years. Since he was a boy he has dreamed of building a successful business. He works up to a point of getting serious about an opportunity and then backs off and stays in the comfortable routine of his job. He is beginning to wonder if he will ever make the commitment.*

Starting a business, whether it is an independent one, a franchise, or a business opportunity takes an enormous amount of initiative. If you have not done it before, it is easy not to start. That's Sean's problem. There are mental obstacles at every turn. You can fall into a trap of indecision, where you constantly search for the exact business of your dreams but never seem to find it. People you love and respect can talk you out of it. You can be discouraged by the doom and gloom of the popular press. You can decide that your route to wealth is working your way up to middle management. There are a thousand reasons not to start.

But you know in your heart that the world rewards courage and persistence.

So start! Make that call. Contact your support team. Start lining up you money resources. Go to that trade show. Ask those questions, and present yourself in the finest light possible to your new business contacts.

You will be pleasantly surprised at how your hard work and persistence pays off, and the interesting places your initiative can lead you. If the words in this book help you take that first step, then you have made my day.

Good luck in your new business!

ACTION PLAN
There is no substitute for taking action. No amount of dreaming, planning, or talking takes its place. If you want to be in business for yourself, you must make it happen. Take action today.

STATE FRANCHISE RELATIONSHIP LAWS

*T*hese states have statutes which may supersede the franchise agreement you have with the franchisor. They typically impose a vaguely defined "good cause" requirement before a franchisor can terminate a relationship during the term of the contract or refuse to renew the contractual term of the franchise.

ARKANSAS [Stat. section 70-807]

CALIFORNIA [Bus. & Prof. Code sections 20000-20043]

CONNECTICUT [Gen. Stat. section 42-133e et seq.]

DELAWARE [Code, tit. 6, ch. 25, Section 2551 et seq.]

DISTRICT OF COLUMBIA [Franchising Act of 1988, DC Code Ann. Sec. 29-1201 to -1208 (1989)]

HAWAII [Rev. Stat. section 482E-1]

ILLINOIS [815 ILCS 705/19 and 705/20]

INDIANA [Stat. section 23-2-2.7]

IOWA [Code sections 523H.1-523H.17]

MICHIGAN [Stat. section 19.854(27)]

MINNESOTA [Stat. section 80C.14]

MISSISSIPPI [Code section 75-24-51]

MISSOURI [Stat. section 407.400]

NEBRASKA [Rev. Stat. section 87-401]

NEW JERSEY [Stat. section 56:10-1]

SOUTH DAKOTA [Codified Laws section 37-5A-51]

VIRGINIA [Code 13.1-557-574-13.1-564]

WASHINGTON [Code section 19.100.180]

WISCONSIN [Stat. section 135.03]

STATE FRANCHISE AUTHORITIES

CALIFORNIA

CALIFORNIA DEPARTMENT OF CORPORATIONS
The Commissioner of Corporations
Department of Corporations
320 West 4th Street
Los Angeles, CA 90013

HAWAII

BUSINESS REGISTRATION DIVISION
Securities Compliance
Department of Commerce and Consumer Affairs
1010 Richards Street
Honolulu, HI 96813

ILLINOIS

FRANCHISE DIVISION OFFICE OF THE ATTORNEY GENERAL
Chief, Franchise Division
Office of the Attorney General
500 South Second Street
Springfield, IL 62706

INDIANA

SECURITIES COMMISSIONER
Indiana Securities Division
Room E 111, 302 West Washington Street
Indianapolis, IN 46204

MARYLAND

OFFICE OF THE ATTORNEY GENERAL
Securities Division
200 St. Paul Place, 20th Floor
Baltimore, MD 21202-2020

MICHIGAN

ANTITRUST AND FRANCHISE UNIT
DEPARTMENT OF THE ATTORNEY GENERAL
Director, Consumer Protection Division
670 Law Building
Lansing, MI 48913

MINNESOTA

THE COMMISSIONER OF COMMERCE
MINNESOTA DEPARTMENT OF COMMERCE
85 7thPlace East, Suite 500
St. Paul, MN 55101-2198

NEW YORK

NEW YORK STATE DEPARTMENT OF LAW
Bureau of Investor Protection and Securities
120 Broadway, 23rd Floor
New York, NY 10271

NORTH DAKOTA

THE COMMISSIONER OF SECURITIES
NORTH DAKOTA OFFICE OF SECURITIES COMMISSIONER
Office of the Securities Commissioner
600 East Boulevard, Fifth Floor
Bismarck, ND 58505

RHODE ISLAND

RHODE ISLAND DIVISION OF SECURITIES
Director, Division of Securities
233 Richmond Street, Suite 232
Providence, RI 02903

SOUTH DAKOTA

SOUTH DAKOTA DIVISION OF SECURITIES
Director, Division of Securities
118 West Capitol
Pierre, SD 57501

VIRGINIA

STATE CORPORATION COMMISSION
DIVISION OF SECURITIES AND RETAIL FRANCHISING
1300 East Main Street, 9th Floor
Richmond, VA 23219

WASHINGTON

DEPARTMENT OF FINANCIAL INSTITUTIONS
Department of Financial Institutions
Securities Division
P.O. Box 9033
Olympia, WA 98507-9033

WISCONSIN

THE COMMISSIONER OF SECURITIES
WISCONSIN SECURITIES COMMISSION
P.O. Box 1768
Madison, WI 53701

OTHER
INFORMATION SOURCES

FTC INFORMATION

Contact the Federal Trade Commission (FTC) for general investment information if you are interested in buying a franchise or business opportunity venture. The Web site is well worth a visit, and the FTC encourages investors to contact the agency if they discover an unlawful franchise practice.

Internet: www.ftc.gov (a great site)

Phone: Consumer Response Center at (202) 326-3128

Fax: (202) 326-2012, Attn: Consumer Response Center

E-mail: consumerline@ftc.gov

U.S. Mail: Federal Trade Commission

                Attn: Consumer Response Center

                Washington, DC 20580

PRIVATE SOURCES

If you don't live in a registration state, or anywhere near the location of the regulators where the documents are on file, you can order a UFOC on file anywhere in the U.S. by calling FranData in Washington DC, at (800) 793-8640. It is a document retrieval business specializing in franchise documents and can sell you any publicly available disclosure document, with prices beginning at $100.

BETTER BUSINESS BUREAU

Look for your local office of the Better Business Bureau in the phone book or on the Web.

STATE FRANCHISE AND BUSINESS OPPORTUNITY LAWS

State	Business Opportunity Law?	Franchise Investment Law?	Franchise Relationship Law?
Alabama	Yes	No	No
Alaska	No	No	No
Arizona	No	No	No
Arkansas	No	No	Yes
California	Yes	Yes	Yes
Colorado	No	No	No
Connecticut	Yes	No	Yes
Delaware	No	No	Yes
District of Columbia	No	No	Yes
Florida	Yes	No	No
Georgia	Yes	No	No
Hawaii	No	Yes	Yes
Idaho	No	No	No
Illinois	Yes	Yes	Yes

State	Business Opportunity Law?	Franchise Investment Law?	Franchise Relationship Law?
Indiana	Yes	Yes	Yes
Iowa	Yes	No	Yes
Kansas	No	No	No
Kentucky	Yes	No	No
Louisiana	Yes	No	No
Maine	Yes	No	No
Maryland	Yes	Yes	No
Massachusetts	No	No	No
Michigan	Yes	Yes	Yes
Minnesota	Yes	Yes	Yes
Mississippi	No	No	Yes
Missouri	No	No	Yes
Montana	No	No	No
Nebraska	Yes	No	Yes
Nevada	No	No	No
New Hampshire	Yes	No	No
New Jersey	No	No	Yes
New Mexico	No	No	No
New York	No	Yes	No
North Carolina	Yes	No	No
North Dakota	No	Yes	No
Ohio	Yes	No	No
Oklahoma	Yes	No	No
Oregon	No	No	No
Pennsylvania	No	No	No

State	Business Opportunity Law?	Franchise Investment Law?	Franchise Relationship Law?
Rhode Island	No	Yes	No
South Carolina	Yes	No	No
South Dakota	Yes	Yes	Yes
Tennessee	No	No	No
Texas	Yes	No	No
Utah	Yes	No	No
Vermont	No	No	No
Virginia	Yes	Yes	Yes
Washington	Yes	Yes	Yes
West Virginia	No	No	No
Wisconsin	No	Yes	Yes
Wyoming	No	No	No

GLOSSARY

Arbitration. Formal dispute resolution process that is legally binding on the parties.

Business Format Franchise. See the definition of "franchise."

Business Opportunity. A package of goods and materials that enables the buyer to begin or maintain a business. The Federal Trade Commission and 25 states regulate the concept.

Copyright. The legal right protecting an original work of authorship that is fixed in a tangible form.

Earnings Claim. A statement by a franchisor regarding the financial performance of existing franchisees or a projection of how a particular investor/franchisee will perform. Earnings claims may be made by a franchisor, but if so, they must be presented in item 19 of the UFOC.

Federal Trade Commission's Franchise Rule. The 1979 trade regulation rule by which all franchisors in the United States are required to deliver a presale disclosure document.

First Personal Meeting. A disclosure trigger under the Federal Trade Commission Rule; not a casual or chance meeting but a detailed discussion about a specific franchise opportunity.

Franchise. The law defines a franchise as the presence of three factors: (1) the grant of trademark rights, (2) a prescribed marketing plan, or significant control or assistance in the operation, or a community of interest, and (3) payment of a franchise fee for the right to participate. In business terms, the franchisee receives full training in the operation, follows a detailed set of business techniques, uses the franchisor's trademark, and pays a continuing royalty for participation in the program.

Franchise Agreement. The contract by which a franchisor grants franchise rights to a franchisee.

Franchisee. One who receives the rights to a franchise. The owner and operator of a franchised business.

Franchise Fee. The money a franchisee is required to pay for the right to participate in the franchise program. Under the federal rules the minimum amount of franchise fee payment allowed before disclosure is required is $500. A franchise fee includes any lump sum initial payment and ongoing royalty payments.

Franchise Investment Laws. The laws of the Federal Trade Commission and 14 states that regulate the sale of a franchise.

Franchise Relationship Laws. State franchise statutes in 19 jurisdictions that generally restrict terminations or nonrenewals of franchise agreements in the absence of "good cause." See appendix A.

Franchisor. The person or company that grants franchise rights to a franchisee.

Limited Liability Company. A relatively new form of business organization with the liability-shield advantages of a corporation and the flexibility and tax pass-through advantages of a partnership.

Mediation. Professionally assisted negotiation. Now frequently used as a first step to resolve a dispute between a franchisor and franchisee. Mediation is generally nonbinding, unless the parties agree to a resulting settlement.

Patent. An inventor's right protecting an invention, new device, or innovation.

Product Franchise. The legal definition is the same as a "franchise." In business terms, it is a system for the distribution of a particular line of products, usually manufactured and/or supplied by the franchisor.

Renewal. Most franchise agreements grant the franchisee the right to renew the initial contract term for additional time at the end of the initial term. The contract may impose conditions on the right to renew, such as providing timely written notice, signing a new form of agreement, and paying a renewal fee.

Royalty Fee. The continuing payment paid by a franchisee to the franchisor. Usually calculated as a percentage of the franchisee's gross sales.

Territory. The rights granted to a franchisee that offer a restriction on competition within a stated area.

Trademark. A word, phrase, or logo design that identifies the source or quality of a product. A service mark means the same thing, but identifies a service.

Trade Show. An exhibition of businesses offering franchises and/or business opportunity packages.

Transfer. The sale of franchise rights by a franchisee to the buyer of all or a portion of the franchisee's business.

UFOC. Uniform Franchise Offering Circular, the specialized franchise disclosure statement that franchisors must deliver to prospective franchisees at the earlier of (1) the first personal meeting for the purpose of discussing the sale or possible sale of a franchise, or (2) ten business days before the prospect signs a franchise agreement or pays money for the right to be a franchisee.

INDEX